'A very important book, based on a very important and impressing research project. Highly recommended.'

Pim van Lommel, *cardiologist, NDE-researcher,*
author of Consciousness Beyond Life

'*Forgiveness and Reconciliation* is a profound and at times deeply moving reflection and study of these key spiritual themes. The author shows how in our capacity as relational beings these processes are catalysed by the imminence of death and how we are affected by unresolved issues and estranged relationships. Based on her research, she formulates a five-stage model, illustrating these phases with intense personal stories that give rise to significant reflections in the reader as we consider how such situations are reflected in our own lives and relationships. At a time of deep divisions this book conveys an essential message of hope and encouragement to engage in our own challenges of forgiveness and reconciliation – and achieve a measure of inner peace in the process.'

David Lorimer, *Programme Director,*
Editor, Paradigm Explorer

Forgiveness and Reconciliation

This book details a five-phase model of the process of forgiveness and reconciliation, exploring how it can be understood as a threshold experience with the potential to offer profound emotional renewal.

Illustrated with numerous case study vignettes, the book presents the findings of a research study gathered from observing and interviewing 50 dying persons, investigating the preconditions for forgiveness and reconciliation, and examining how a sense of grace, freedom, peace, and deep connectedness may occur. The book also contextualizes reconciliation and forgiveness as cultural phenomena extending beyond purely behavioral patterns of cooperation and involving great emotional maturity and strength of personality.

Centered on humility, self-knowledge, truth-finding, and consciousness, *Forgiveness and Reconciliation* is important reading for practitioners, scholars and students in the fields of counseling, psychotherapy, and palliative care and to all those interested in supporting people in conflict situations in the middle of their lives or in working with dying persons.

Monika Renz is a psychotherapist, music therapist, and spiritual caregiver. She leads the psycho-oncology unit at a clinic of oncology/hematology (Cantonal Hospital of St. Gallen, Switzerland). She holds a PhD in psychopathology and in theology/spirituality and is an internationally sought speaker and author of several books. Her research focuses on dying, spirituality, forgiveness, and fear.

Routledge Focus on Mental Health

Routledge Focus on Mental Health presents short books on current topics, linking in with cutting-edge research and practice.

The Working Alliance in Rational Emotive Behaviour Therapy: Principles and Practice
Windy Dryden

Psychoanalysis and Euripides' Suppliant Women: A Tragic Reading of Politics
Sotiris Manolopoulos

The Gifts We Receive from Animals: Stories to Warm the Heart
Lori R. Kogan

James Joyce and the Internal World of the Replacement Child
Mary Adams

Analytic Listening in Clinical Dialogue: Basic Assumptions
Dieter Bürgin, Angelika Staehle, Kerstin Westhoff, and Anna Wyler von Ballmoos

Growing Through the Erotic Transference: An Analysand's Journey
Frances H. Moore

Treatment for Body-Focused Repetitive Behaviors: An Integrative Psychodynamic Approach
Stacy K. Nakell

For a full list of titles in this series, please visit https://www.routledge.com/Routledge-Focus-on-Mental-Health/book-series/RFMH

Forgiveness and Reconciliation
Initiating Individuation and Enabling Liberation

Monika Renz

Translated by Mark Kyburz

LONDON AND NEW YORK

First published 2023
by Routledge
4 Park Square, Milton Park, Abingdon, Oxon OX14 4RN

and by Routledge
605 Third Avenue, New York, NY 10158

Routledge is an imprint of the Taylor & Francis Group, an informa business

© 2023 Monika Renz

The right of Monika Renz to be identified as author of this work has been asserted in accordance with sections 77 and 78 of the Copyright, Designs and Patents Act 1988.

All rights reserved. No part of this book may be reprinted or reproduced or utilised in any form or by any electronic, mechanical, or other means, now known or hereafter invented, including photocopying and recording, or in any information storage or retrieval system, without permission in writing from the publishers.

Trademark notice: Product or corporate names may be trademarks or registered trademarks, and are used only for identification and explanation without intent to infringe.

British Library Cataloguing-in-Publication Data
A catalogue record for this book is available from the British Library

Library of Congress Cataloguing-in-Publication Data
Names: Renz, Monika, 1961- author. | Kyburz, Mark, 1963- translator.
Title: Forgiveness and reconciliation : initiating individuation and enabling liberation / Monika Renz ; translated by Mark Kyburz.
Description: New York, NY : Routledge, 2023. | Series: Routledge focus on mental health | Includes bibliographical references and index. |
Identifiers: LCCN 2022018453 | ISBN 9781032316970 (hardback) | ISBN 9781032316987 (paperback) | ISBN 9781003310907 (ebook)
Subjects: LCSH: Forgiveness. | Reconciliation.
Classification: LCC BF637.F67 R4613 2023 | DDC 155.9/2--dc23/eng/20220614
LC record available at https://lccn.loc.gov/2022018453

ISBN: 978-1-032-31697-0 (hbk)
ISBN: 978-1-032-31698-7 (pbk)
ISBN: 978-1-003-31090-7 (ebk)

DOI: 10.4324/9781003310907

Typeset in Times New Roman
by MPS Limited, Dehradun

Contents

List of Illustrations ix
Acknowledgments x

**Introduction: What is reconciliation, and what is
forgiveness?** 1
*The Historical and religio-historical backgrounds of
reconciliation and forgiveness 5*
*Pilot study: "Forgiveness and reconciliation processes in
dying patients with cancer" 8*

1 Why reconciliation? Why forgiveness? 14

1.1 *Are we free to forgive? 14*
1.2 *What motivates us to engage in the process? 17*
1.3 *Before major life transitions: The opportunity of
being close to death 18*
1.4 *Forgiveness and reconciliation as an expression of
strength 23*
1.5 *What if the other side refuses? 25*
1.6 *Unreconciled conflicts affect us as relational
beings 25*

2 The need for perspective 30

2.1 *Reconciliation and forgiveness happen after
category change 30*
2.2 *Spaces of feeling 32*

viii *Contents*

    2.3   Conscious realization, post-maturation, truth-finding 32

    2.4   Reconciliation and forgiveness begin with new empathy 35

    2.5   Renunciation, waiting, trusting: Overcoming hard times 39

    2.6   How realistic is reconciliation as a mutual process? 40

    2.7   Third parties enable reconciliation and forgiveness 42

    2.8   Risking vulnerability: The significance of scapegoating 45

    2.9   What do victims need? 48

    2.10   What do perpetrators need? 52

    2.11   Forgiveness as decision: Two models from the victim's perspective 55

    2.12   Deliverance from guilt: Two models from the perpetrator's perspective 58

3   The five-phase reconciliation process   64

    3.1   Denial or avoidance 64

    3.2   Crisis 67

    3.3   Experiences of hope (or the factor of grace) 72

    3.4   Decision 74

    3.5   Reconciliation and forgiveness 78

4   It happens where regret and grace meet   84

    References   87

    Appendix   91

    Index   95

Illustrations

Figures

A1	Patient 5: Trajectory and conflicts	91
A2	Patient 60: Trajectory and conflicts	92
A3	Subcategories of forgiveness/ reconciliation (Phase 5)	93

Tables

3.1	Denial (Kübler-Ross: denial)	66
3.2	Crisis (Kübler-Ross: anger)	71
3.3	Experience of hope, motivation, something encourages reconciliation	73
3.4	Decision, determination: Patient addresses the issue	77
A1	Characteristics of sample	94

Acknowledgments

I am indebted to many people for supporting me and the cause to which I am committed: Dr. Mark Kyburz (my translator), Dr. med. Daniel Büche, Dr. Miriam Schütt Mao, Oliver Reichmuth, Claudio Gloggner, Anne Duveen, Dr. med. Gisela Leyting, Regina Stillhart, Lilo Bohnenblust, Dr. med. Urs Ruegg, Prof. Paul Zulehner, Prof. Roman Siebenrock, my superior Prof. Christoph Driessen, my mother Helen Renz, and my husband Jürg. I wish to thank Emilie Coin and Alexis O'Brien at Routledge for their interest in this book and its approach. I am grateful to the many patients entrusted to me for their trust and for sharing their process. I thank what cannot be thanked and yet "is" grace, creative energy—God.

Introduction: What is reconciliation, and what is forgiveness?

Reconciliation is an unwieldly word. It means more than coming to terms with others—and also more than mere scheming or strategizing. The Middle High German word *versuenen* means to make peace, to mediate, and to settle conflicts. It is related to atonement, that is, to make amends. Thus, unsurprisingly, we seldom use the word "reconciliation" in everyday life. And yet, it calls for attention, as the subject on which it touches is existential and frequent, in particular as we approach death. Do we suppress reconciliation for as long as possible? And if so, why? As a rule, reconciliation involves forgiveness, which proves emotionally difficult—and yet liberating.

This is exactly what my father tried to teach me from an early age. He told me about situations in his life where he had managed to say "yes"—to a quarrelsome sister, or to a hot-tempered co-worker, whom he assigned special tasks and thus involved more actively in the company. After reconciling or shaking hands, my father added, things were not just fine (i.e., resolved) between him and the other person, but freer. After all, he had not wanted the disagreement to burden him for half a lifetime. Several months after our conversation—I had not forgotten its contents—I asked my father how things had continued ... and realized they no longer mattered to him. He had forgotten.

My father has since passed. He was peace-loving, impulsive and insistent, because he was so sincere. After a dispute, he was always first to offer his hand to make amends, to seek reconciliation. World history, he said, provided many great role models who had struggled to achieve peace and reconciliation: former Egyptian statesman Anwar as-Sadat, or the black South African bishop Desmond Tutu at the end of the apartheid regime.

Forgiveness and reconciliation are parting gifts—threshold experiences. Before a major life change, and as we look ahead to new things, we are able to bring to completion our life, or a special period of our

DOI: 10.4324/9781003310907-1

2 Introduction

life, or indeed a life theme—and to forgive, to let matters rest. These processes occur during radical change. This is true especially for the threshold to death. We need to understand radical forgiveness and reconciliation in terms of death! Or in terms of a completely new stage of life—that is, with Jesus and his resurrection in mind. Why?

As we approach death, the previously unthinkable occurs. Not just for some of us, but for most of us. There—as one doctor tried to explain to the relative of a dying patient—ancient brain-physiological initiations and false initiations open up. Hardened feelings soften. Everything begins flowing so powerfully that—on a primary, sensitive level—we have not been as "alive" for a long time as we are at that very moment. In supporting many dying persons, I have observed that death does not occur when we stiffen or grow rigid, but rather when we are open within ourselves.

This profound openness is where reconciliation and forgiveness *simply take place*. It happens near death, yet also when renewal occurs so deeply in the middle of life that even age-old misguided ideas, as mentioned above, are left behind. In Christian terms, this is what Easter stands for. Then, what was previously impossible becomes possible. It is no coincidence that Jesus only rarely proclaimed forgiveness and reconciliation during his lifetime—yet did so, both naturally and emphatically, as the Risen Lord.

This raises the question about my own spirituality. I am an open-minded religious person, a practising Christian, and attracted to the combination of various fields: religious studies, the depth psychology of C.G. Jung, Erich Neumann and Stanislav Grof, and music therapy. My spirituality is influenced by my studies in theology as well as in depth psychology and ethnomusicology, where I focused on healing rituals in different ethnic groups. I often have in-depth discussions and conversations with agnostics, who are not adverse to discussing my approach to religion (Renz 2017), to human development (see my *Fear and Primordial Trust*, 2022), and to dying (see my *Dying: A Transition*, 2015). My deepest formative experiences occurred during bouts of illness when I was young and later after several accidents. What I experienced was similar to a near-death experience and enhanced my sensitivity for spiritual experience, and also for music and vibration. I also work with patients from different cultural backgrounds, where reconciliation and forgiveness also play a central role in how people become who they are (see, e.g., Bassam Ramadani, Section 1.1). Nonetheless, all end-of-life care needs to address the question of bias time and again (for the limitations of my research, see below).

Introduction 3

Despite its radical subject—forgiveness and reconciliation processes—this book—even when it concerns the process of dying—is not about death, but rather about coming to life. It is about the chance to forgive and reconcile, and about how both forgiveness and reconciliation function as a "gateway" to new life. It is about understanding forgiveness and reconciliation as profound processes, and about what enables us to engage in them and why they are worthwhile.

What is the difference between reconciliation and forgiveness? Reconciliation is relational. It describes the path to restoring peace and order between hostile parties. In contrast, forgiveness usually takes place in the depths of our own soul. While the term forgiveness refers to a gift and a giver, reconciliation emphasizes repentance, atonement and the moment of transformation. Strictly, reconciliation means the process of purification (catharsis, reformation) in the perpetrator that enables the victim to forgive. Concretely, however, the positions of victim and perpetrator are never clearly separable. In everyday life, reconciliation always involves victims *and* perpetrators, who are both challenged in their own particular way. These processes, moreover, often proceed in the reverse direction: Forgiveness is what makes reconciliation possible in the first place.

Forgiveness is the step taken by one side (Gerl-Falkovitz, 2008, p. 174), and thus creates a new beginning. Involving more than settling accounts, this "gift" heralds a category change: from having to being. Whereas previously we behaved like prisoners, clinging to our possessions, constantly eyeing them, yet also justifying having them, these "terms of ownership" and "accounts" no longer apply afterwards. We have left them behind, now feeling more relaxed and freer as a result (Section 2.1).

Forgiveness happens when we persevere, wrestle, and seek resolution. It also means to pardon. These concepts are closely related. Pardoning emphasizes allegation, accusation.[1] But instead of accusing something or someone, we extricate ourselves from the sinister cycle of retribution. Everyday language prefers to speak of forgiveness, for instance, when resolving relationship problems reasonably straightforward (Herzog, 2017, p. 19).

Forgiveness, moreover, refers more to the gift and the given: Being able to forgive is also a matter of grace—which probably explains why I find it more appealing. Forgiveness involves unconditional affirmation: saying "yes" to others, to myself, to life, to destiny, and ultimately to God. As this is profoundly challenging, we must *really and truly decide to forgive* (see Enright's model in Section 2.11). Not only that: We must take this decision time and again.

4   *Introduction*

What about reconciliation? Taking decisions is also integral to the reconciliation process. Working in psycho-oncology for over 20 years at St. Gallen Cantonal Hospital, I have often come across patients who willfully *decided* to tackle reconciliation head-on and who accepted therapeutic support with this intention in mind.

Processes close to death represent a special case: They take place faster and often remain fragmentary. Hence, a person's decisions are not always evident to others. Still, these processes are no less liberating and intensive (Section 1.3). Saying "yes" to what was may occur imperceptibly, for instance, when breathing out, through a physical "jolt," in a softening gaze or a relaxing muscle tone.

What, however, makes us emotionally able to decide to forgive or to take concrete steps towards reconciliation? The inconceivable happens when I manage to reach beyond myself or when I am deeply motivated, for instance, by a role model or by a deep or sustaining experience of hope or grace (Chapter 2 and Section 3.3). In this book, the experience of hope constitutes a distinct phase in the reconciliation process. This particular emphasis is new in the discussion of forgiveness and reconciliation. Even in dying, indeed precisely then, we can hope beyond ourselves. It becomes clear how important this is both for the dying person and for achieving peace in their surroundings.

Thus, do forgiveness and reconciliation presuppose hope? Yes, even if hope remains hidden in another, "different category of being" (Section 2.1). Hope often resurges when another, a third person appreciates my hurt and conflicts. Ultimately, hope enables what seems impossible. Without deep hope, and amid suffering, we are long *unable* to honestly forgive extreme hurt or achieve reconciliation.

The moment of forgiveness within the reconciliation process not only presupposes hope but also *creates* it. Even in the midst of resignation, traumatic blockages, and despair, the path of forgiveness—whenever it occurs—once again makes something new possible. With the act of forgiveness, hope is reborn as it were, and becomes tangibly "present." All of a sudden, our thinking has a different thrust: No longer gravitating around an "if-then," or "entrapped" within logical reasoning, our mind opens up and asks: "What next?"

This future orientation creates a new atmosphere, one which enables the dying to say that "things are good as they are." For us as relatives, it means we enjoy their company. Their attitude of forgiveness lends the dying a very special, "beautiful" charisma. This also occurs when a dying person burdened with severe guilt has gained inner peace and is convinced that the person they once wronged will at some stage forgive them.

What about reconciliation? While I can approach forgiveness alone—within myself—reconciliation as a rule depends on someone else. Often, it must be deferred indefinitely—and deposited with a third person or with God or the Supreme Being (in this respect, I also speak of unilateral reconciliation; see Sections 1.5 and 2.7). The old Hebrew term *shaphat* ("to pronounce sentence, God is the judge") implies that this third person may also be God or the Supreme Being. Achieving reconciliation with the help of a third person or with God is itself an act of hope as that this third party provides courage and motivation.

The historical and religio-historical backgrounds of reconciliation and forgiveness

Historically, thinking in terms of guilt and reconciliation refers us especially to the Judeo-Christian tradition. There, reconciliation is an ancient practice and marks out the path to God's forgiveness. It involves restoring the original connectedness between God and humans, which at some point was interrupted in the course of human evolution and development. This is the original meaning of "sin" (Renz, 2017; see also my *Jesus The Mystic: Pathways to Spiritual Care*, 2020). Reconciliation is the opposite of the ancient concept of sin: Reconciliation heals us from sin. This, in turn, we need to understand as separation, as the dissociation of human beings from God and from their primordial ground. It describes the severing or disruption of this fundamental relationship and goes hand in hand with our departure from the depths of our souls. According to C.G. Jung, "sin" corresponds to a broken or nonexistent ego-self axis. Reconciliation, then, reconnects us with our psychic depths.

Interestingly, the German word *Versöhnung* has two meanings in English. While "reconciliation" describes restoring amicable, benevolent, and conciliatory relations—among and through people—the little-used term "atonement" refers to the God–human relationship, which needs to be restored.[2] According to old convictions, one also had to do with the other.

In a religio-historical and biblical view, the meaning of reconciliation underwent a particular development.[3] In the past, people believed that human beings needed atonement and repentance to "change God's mind"—for instance, in Moses's atoning sacrifice (Ex 29:41) or in the rite of reconciliation (Lev 16:9; Lev 20–22). Gradually, God's readiness to forgive was regarded increasingly as pure grace—as "unpurchasable" (see the Reformation's concept of *sola gratia*, "by grace alone").

6 Introduction

At the same time, people's willingness to reconcile and forgive one another became more important. This tendency is already evident in the Old Testament, for instance, in Jesus Sirach.[4] It is even more notable in the New Testament, in Jesus's behavior, or in the Lord's prayer: "Forgive us our trespasses, as we forgive those who trespass against us."

In other, non-biblical religions, the terms reconciliation and forgiveness do not exist. Well, at least not in this original categorial sense, even if the question about restoring the cosmic order plays a role in those religions in its own particular way. Neither "reconciliation" nor "forgiveness" appears in standard reference works, for instance, the *Handbuch religionswissenschaftlicher Grundbegriffe* (Cancik, Gadigow & Laubscher, 1988) or in the *Encyclopedia of Religion* (Eliade, 1993), perhaps "because unlike in Judaism and Christianity paths to salvation do not begin with God's reconciliatory action towards humankind."[5]

In Islam, we find the idea that the merciful God forgives transgression, after remorse has been shown and penance done (i.e., after amends have been made).[6] This, too, gives rise to a corresponding attitude: "We should live forgiving and hoping for forgiveness," as Mohammed commends the Muslims (Karimi in Grün & Karimi, 2019, p. 31). Buddhism emphasizes compassion, for example, in a form of mediation known as *Metta*, which means kindness, infinite goodness, and taking an active interest in others. This practice resonates not directly but indirectly with a reconciliatory and forgiving stance. Hawaiians have a religious ritual—*Hoʻoponopono*—that is interpreted as seeking reconciliation with the ancestors. Michael McCullough, a professor of psychology, has found indications or evidence of conflict resolution rites in 56 out of 60 human cultures.[7] Whether reconciliation is the right word for these phenomena probably needs to be discussed case-by-case.

Since the onset of modernity, the idea of a "forgiving" God, who "actively initiates reconciliation," has dissipated increasingly. The concepts of humankind and God have changed, as has the meaning of reconciliation. This became a humanistic concern, as sugggested by the Truth Commission in South Africa or the process of coming to terms with the crimes perpetrated during the Holocaust in Germany. Reconciliation manifested in political, psychotherapeutic, and spiritually oriented peace work.[8] Over time, various therapy concepts (Worthington, 2006; Enright, 2001; Stauss 2010; von Tiedemann, 2017) and spiritual paths to reconciliation, such as the Prayer of the Heart and the pilgrimage culture around the Camino de Santiago, have been developed.

Introduction 7

Waning religiosity has coincided with the emergence of new ideas of the divine, of the Whole, also under the influence of research on quantum physics and near-death experiences (van Lommel, 2010). The highest, supreme power is now conceived of—depending on personal background—as being, as relationship, or as energy. It can be experienced in both of its aspects (being and relationship; Renz, 2016). Claiming an ultimate connectedness, according to which human beings participate in such a Whole, has thus become legitimate also in the secularized world. Into this fits research on behavioral patterns oriented towards de-escalation, association, and compassion, which are deeply ingrained in human beings, their genes,[9] and partly also in animals.

The primatologist Frans de Waal, for instance, observed that chimpanzees and bonobos exchange friendly gestures again after being locked in aggressive conflicts; he also noted that these animals display not only vengeful reactions but also cooperative ones.[10] McCullough (2008) found cooperative patterns of behavior in chimpanzees, goats, sheep, dolphins, and other animals. Contrary to self-preservation, these patterns serve to maintain group relationships (pp. 119–120, 130–132). The *human being* is oriented even more towards a "You"; we need only consider the importance of their first attachment figures for children and their development.

Thus, are human beings ultimately oriented towards deep relatedness and connectedness? Does another, similarly profound striving exist alongside our urge towards isolation and self-assertion? A longing for relationship, peace, community, connectedness? This claim is daring in itself—and yet explosive in the context of this book. Accordingly, reconciliation amounts to more than seeking remedy and correction in conflicts. It corresponds to human nature![11]

The neuroscientist and psychiatrist Joachim Bauer has argued along similar lines: Contemplating forgiveness is feasible only in terms of a concept of humankind that is based on ultimate connectedness (cited in Stauss, 2010, p. 11). If, on the other hand, human beings, Darwinistically speaking, were determined solely by aggression and selection, reconciliation and forgiveness would run counter to human nature. As human beings, we can be determined by *both* forces: by the urge for isolation and for a powerful ego (instinctual aggression in Darwin's sense), yet also by a deep longing for connectedness that is hard to define. Following Richard Rohr (2012) and Pim van Lommel (2010), this is how I understand "connectedness."

Reconciliation and forgiveness are cultural phenomena. They elude purely biological thinking. Thus, it strikes me as questionable that "reconciliation"[12] is used to describe neurobiological or instinctive

8 *Introduction*

reactions as well as group-preservation strategies. I would not speak of "reconciliation" on the level of instinct, but rather of instinctual orientations and of cooperative behavior patterns. Such patterns can be fundamental for emotional, cultural, and spiritual development to the point of achieving actual reconciliation and forgiveness.

The latter, however, as this book shows time and again, involves greater emotional maturity, strength of personality, and determination than exists on the level of instinct. Reconciliation and forgiveness concern humility, self-knowledge, truth-finding, and becoming conscious. They somehow presuppose a certain awareness. But what about the dying? How far can, or indeed must, we speak of emotional maturity, consciousness, and culpability in their case? (Section 2.3).

This book combines theoretical and practical approaches, humanistic and spiritual thinking, which have grown and evolved over 20 years of practising psycho-oncology at a central hospital. Individual fates are as much a part of this book as the results of empirical research. What follows is aimed at specialists supporting people in conflict situations in the middle of their lives or working with dying persons. It also addresses readers who wish to engage with its concerns in their own lives. And it intends to encourage people to dare reconciliation processes, whatever the obstacles and opportunities.

Pilot study: "Forgiveness and reconciliation processes in dying patients with cancer"

This book is based on a study titled "Forgiveness and Reconciliation Processes in Dying Patients with Cancer." During my twenty years at St. Gallen Cantonal Hospital, I have met many patients who showed signs in this direction: reconciliation with a loved one, reconciliation with illness and themselves, with fate and God. Our small team of experts[13] wanted to better understand these processes.

How do different people deal with the unreconciled within themselves and around them? This question moved our patients for weeks, months, or even years, between which shorter or longer interruptions occurred (for sample trajectories, see Appendix). While reconciliation remained present in some patients up to the speechlessness immediately before death, the vast majority of dying patients addressed this theme (Section 1.3; Appendix).

How, then, can we, as end-of-life carers, support the dying in this process—with utmost respect, reverent restraint, and the necessary courage? Thus confronted, what should we articulate and how? Can we expose ourselves? A broad range of issues surfaced in our study,

Introduction 9

involving people who had committed violence under the influence of alcohol alongside victims of domestic violence. Serious accusations and projections alongside self-accusations or the simple concern for a forgotten person or for someone who disappeared from a family's consciousness. Issues that ran in families: One patient committed a white-collar crime, just as his father and grandfather had done in their village. Another patient repeatedly cheated on her husband, as was common in her family. Another, depressive patient, had abused her children and finally given them away; she had suffered the same fate as a child at the hands of her single mother. Another patient came from a family whose members had committed suicide for generations. Not infrequently, such severe family issues coincided with an aversion to God.

What interested us most were not only the content and background of conflicts, but also the *inner dynamics of processes of reconciliation and forgiveness.* What inhibits us, what drives us? What do we find extremely difficult, what easy? And, if so, when and under which conditions? What opens us up or eventually leads us to peace? Can we distinguish phases within such processes? Can we speak of a process at all?

I have developed a five-phase model of forgiveness/reconciliation: *denial—crisis—experience of hope—decision—reconciliation/transformation/relaxation* (Sections 3.1–3.5). Reconciliation (phase 5) was experienced in different nuances: It seldom merely involved release at the expense of a scapegoat, for instance, a doctor. This classifies as pseudo-reconciliation rather than as reconciliation proper. On another occasion, "live and let live" proved to be realistic. In a third, very frequent instance, *inner* reconciliation and forgiveness occurred, while in a fourth, a reconciled reunion with the conflict party became possible.

Like all creative impulses, our model, as well as the nuances of reconciliation, grew from intuition. Nevertheless, our discussions with 20 specialists (physicians, psycho-oncologists, nurses, and one pastor) over the course of a year proved important. In a preliminary project conducted with these experts, we refined and adapted our observation form. During subsequent data collection, we recorded and observed 50 patients (31 men, 19 women) during their process over a period of two and a half years. They all died. A further 10 patients, who did not die, were also evaluated for the purpose of comparison: Did they achieve a similar degree of reconciliation and forgiveness? They, too, had the sword of Damocles, approaching death, hanging over them. This, however, withdrew, and death did not occur for the time being. These patients continued to live. They were also evaluated as to whether conflict and reconciliation had not resurfaced for a period of six months.

10 Introduction

The method resembled that of my earlier studies.[14] Once again, and whenever the dying are concerned, an explosive ethical question arose: How can or how might highly individual processes be captured to the point of speechlessness? The intimacy of the dying process, and the seriousness of the urge for peace before death, forbid any voyeurism, including objectively recording data with the help of questionnaires. Instead, our interdisciplinary team *observed* what occurred with regard to both the lack of reconciliation and the reconciliation process. Observations took place in the hospital's palliative unit, oncological unit, and on an outpatient basis. The study heightened our team's awareness of the need for reconciliation and supportive interventions. After meeting a patient or their family, a semi-structured questionnaire was completed for internal quality control purposes. Whenever interventions proved effective, two to three questionnaires were completed: What happened before, during, and after meetings? We also recorded the after-effects of reconciliation, for instance, when the dying process took its course. Forty-nine percent of those patients who died after reconciliation passed away within less than 48 hours, a further 13% entered peaceful somnolence immediately after reconciliation. Thus, reconciliation processes have a decisive impact—and provide relief.

Our study design was approved by the Government Ethics Committee (EKOS).[15] No informed consent was necessary.[16] The study was based on participant observation, but only caregivers, nurses, and physicians from our institution (St. Gallen Cantonal Hospital) were entitled to collect and pass on data. The case vignettes in this book are included with the consent of the patients concerned or, if deceased, with that of their relatives. All patient details have been anonymized to protect confidentiality.

Our study had several limitations.[17] Nevertheless, the many professionals from different backgrounds and the amount of data (660 observation protocols), in addition to the many qualitatively recorded sentences and sentence fragments uttered by patients, make interpretation possible.

In parallel to data collection, we conducted a thorough literature research. This was followed by close analysis, which required two researchers to reflectively engage with the process and the respective situation. In case of doubt, a third researcher (appointed in advance) was consulted for their interpretation. We studied a wealth of statistical material and discussed interpretations—also with various international experts.

Our study deepened my insight into the importance of reconciliation and forgiveness, as well as my respect for those who dare such processes.

Introduction 11

It raised my awareness of a spiritual urge near death, of the factor of grace, that is, of the small or large invading experiences of hope motivating forgiveness and reconciliation in the first place. And it initiated me into the liberating potential of reconciliation and forgiveness.

In sum:

Forgiveness and reconciliation are breakthroughs.

They serve as gateways.

And we need to think of forgiveness and reconciliation in terms of a final point (death) or in terms of the hope of something radically new in life (e.g., Jesus's Kingdom of Heaven).

And often, such radical turning points in life or at the end of life can make forgiveness and reconciliation possible.

Notes

1 We also need to understand the German word *Verzeihung* (forgiveness) from the victim's perspective, as it resonates with *Bezichtigung* (*zeihen*, Middle High German *zihin*, Old High German *zihan*; *bezichtigen, zeigen auf*, "to accuse," "to point at."

2 Atonement means reconciliation with God. It was used in particular with Jesus's sin offering. That is, when, Jesus's devotion allows us to experience reconnection, that we are once again connected or in one with God or the Supreme Being ("at-one-ment with God"). In its Reformatory sense, the term refers to doing penance.

3 What are my reflections on religion based on? After practising psycho-oncology for several years, and impressed by many encounters with patients, I decided to broaden my background and studied theology at the universities of Zurich (Protestant), Innsbruck and Fribourg (Catholic). My deepest formative experiences, my own patients' deathbed visions and near-death experiences have also influenced my particular approach to theology (see further my *Jesus The Mystic: Pathways to Spiritual Care*, 2020), as several theologians agree: I distinguish three ways of interpreting the various holy scriptures such as the Bible: (1) as words of revelation, written by humans inspired by a holy spirit; (2) many passages need to be interpreted from a historical-critical perspective because they are influenced decisively by their historical context. These two approaches are common, but a third approach needs also to be taken into account; (3) interpreting the holy scriptures on an (archetypal and/or culturally bound) symbolic level that corresponds to dream consciousness rather than to rational everyday consciousness (see the illustrations of psychic layers in my *Fear and Primordial Trust*, 2022, pp. 26–27 and 153). When the various holy scriptures were written, people lived and thought naturally in terms of symbols and metaphors. Exactly this symbolical world seems to be analogous to the experiences and metaphors of the dying. Knowing about them,

12   *Introduction*

and about symbolism in terms of C.G. Jung's approach, helps us to better understand the holy scriptures as well as the specific language of dying patients, also when the dying touch on forgiveness and reconciliation.

4 See the Wisdom of Sirach (28:1–2): "Forgive thy neighbour the hurt that he hath done unto thee, so shall thy sins also be forgiven when thou prayest."

5 Roman Siebenbrock, personal communication.

6 Penance: "al-tauba"; Sūrat Al-Tawbah (: سورة التوبة, "The Repentance") is the title of the ninth chapter of the Koran.

7 Human Relations Area Files, HRAF McCullough, 2008, pp. 121–122.

8 See Lederach (1997) and Galtung (1998).

9 Nowak (2006) considers cooperation part of evolution like mutation and selection. It already occurs on the level of genes, bacteria, and cells.

10 de Waal 2000, p. 16.

11 Similarly to the desire for revenge or food (involving activation of the left prefrontal cortex; McCullough, 2008, pp. 141–142), an opposite development may occur, causing the corresponding cortex activation to subside, among others, when we empathize with someone who has hurt us (McCullough, 2008, p. 149).

12 Primatologists speak of a "conciliatory tendency" in primates' cooperative behavior (McCullough, 2008, p. 119). McCullough makes a similar point about the group behavior of goats, sheep, dolphins, and hyenas (2008, pp. 119–120; 130–132). He also uses the term "reconciliation" for the above-mentioned empathic, cortex-deactivating *human* behavior and contrasts this with the desire for revenge and hunger (2008, p. 149).

13 Besides my research associate Dr. phil. Miriam Schuett Mao and myself, our study team comprised Dr. Daniel Büche (palliative care physician) and Oliver Reichmuth (a male nurse and chemical laboratory technician). We discussed our work with various international experts: Dr. Pim van Lommel (cardiologist and expert on near-death experience), Prof. Dr. Roman Siebenrock (theologian), Prof. Dr. Ursula Renz (philosopher), and PD Dr. Florian Strasser (palliative physician).

14 Data collection: Participant observation. Data analysis: Interpretative phenomenological analysis (individual questions, individual trajectories, considering each patient individually) combined with descriptive statistics (general statements, graphs). On methodology, see also Renz et al. (2018).

15 EKOS approval was granted in accordance with Art. 34 of the Human Research Act of the Swiss Confederation.

16 EKOS justified its decision by stating that it was impossible or disproportionately difficult with this specific cohort to obtain consent. Finally, the interests and benefits of the research outweighed the interests of any persons involved in deciding on the further use of data (Appendix, HRA Art. 34), except for the case vignettes (see above).

17 There were seven limitations:

1   We only studied patients with cancer.

2   Our sample size (see appendix, table 1) did not include patients with a different cultural background, partly by coincidence and partly for language reasons. Thus, we only studied patients with a (secularized) Christian background. However, isolated experiences with patients from other cultures, before or after the recording period, reveal a

Introduction 13

similar explosiveness of the topic (see Bassam Ramadani, Section 1.1). Follow-up studies are necessary.

3 Our observation protocol was developed based on discussions with professionals at our hospital and hence tailored to our patients' needs. However, 20 professionals from different backgrounds (nurses, physicians, therapists, and spiritual caregivers) were involved. Moreover, we ran a one-year pilot.

4 Between observations lay unrecorded periods. Particular phases, especially decisions, may have existed but were not communicated.

5 Observations might be biased by observers' personal attitudes and different professional backgrounds. However, two factors helped reduce individual bias: Our study involved three hospital units and only included patients who were observed by members of at least two professions.

6 The scarcity of comparable studies makes it difficult to conclude which factors may explain different findings.

7 The limited data on NDE/spiritual experiences barely allow drawing conclusions. It remains open whether gender, age, and religiosity significantly affect forgiveness.

For further details on our study, see Renz, M., Bueche, D., Reichmuth, O., Schuett Mao, M., Renz, U., Siebenrock, R., & Strasser, F. (2020). Forgiveness and reconciliation processes in dying patients with cancer. *American Journal of Hospice & Palliative Care*, *37*(3), 222–234. https://doi.org/10.1177/104990911 9867675

1 Why reconciliation?
Why forgiveness?

1.1 Are we free to forgive?

I was watching my four-year-old nephew quarrel with his two-and-a-half-year-old sister. The boy lashed out. A little later their father sat down next to the children and talked to them quite sternly. Afterwards the boy, partly seeing his father's point, wanted to grab his sister's hand and say "sorry." She pulled back, not (yet) wanting to make amends. A little later, during the next game, the father hugged both children. The previous events no longer mattered.

In 20 or 40 years' time, matters will not be quite so simple. Although division becomes rarer in adulthood, it becomes much more serious. Fronts will harden, self-assertion, prestige-seeking and plenty more forbid us from showing signs of weakness and reaching out to others to make peace ... until perhaps at some point a new softness or longing for peace emerges.

Rahel was suffering ever more consciously from the effects of her father's incest. Her brothers had no idea, only one sister knew, had experienced it herself and believed the unbelievable. Rahel kept doubting everything and thus also herself. Then her father died and shortly afterwards her mother. Years later Rahel dreamed about her father asking her for forgiveness. She struggled with the idea. Why should she forgive him? She began struggling whenever the memories or the physical and emotional after-effects caught up with her. Once, during music-assisted relaxation, she heard the strange word "my child." It never let go of her. But she did not understand the message. Then she had an Aha! moment: it had been her father's voice. Rahel was moved. Was she reconciled for an instant?—She is still struggling, ... though at least something has opened up since. When

DOI: 10.4324/9781003310907-2

Why reconciliation? Why forgiveness? 15

will the moment come when she can forgive "in freedom"? And how many times will she have to understand this?

Bassam Ramadani, a Muslim refugee who was quite well integrated in Switzerland and married to a Christian woman, felt uprooted in his advanced illness. Despite his excellent German, he could barely speak to his former colleagues; their world was a different one. He was also increasingly losing the ability to form sentences due to a metastatic brain tumor. He was still emotionally responsive, esteemed my appreciation for him, my music, my spontaneous and free prayer as a Christian, and that I had an idea of what suffering meant. He always came accompanied by his wife. But more and more, even during our therapy sessions, he became as if "taken from himself." A deep chasm separated him from everything: from his successful life trajectory in Switzerland, from his parents, his children, from me as his therapist and probably also from himself. His despair was wordless, boundless. I could only guess how much his past as a refugee was now preoccupying him. How did he cope with this state? His answer overwhelmed me. Only his wife was still present: he no longer felt anything for himself, even food no longer tasted good, but she was still there. He tapped his chest and repeated "heeere." In the midst of this distress, the two of them prayed together, time and again repeating the words "We forgive" in his native language. That did him good. And they began to read the Koran together. Individual suras became like a mantra to him. He understood, even if he didn't understand. The boy from back then understood. And his eyes lit up.

Hildegard was in her 70 s when she told me about a hunch that wouldn't let go of her: she was moving towards something yet had no inkling what it might be. It turned out to be a profound change. Hildegard was urged (several times!) as if from within. Images from her dreams and imagination contained dark violet colours beside bright yellow, a large black bowl kept reappearing, once even with sparks of light inside it. For Hildegard, these images symbolized that she was being carried deeply amid darkness. Months later, she had a dream: she was in a large cathedral in Italy. A small nun approached her and from somewhere Hildegard heard a deep voice say: "Reconciliation needs space and ritual." The dream shook Hildegard. What is forgiveness? Whom did she need to achieve reconciliation with? She now knew that the subject was present.—A few months later, I heard that Hildegard had been admitted to the emergency room and had undergone surgery. She spent two weeks in

16   *Why reconciliation? Why forgiveness?*

the intensive care unit, between life and death. Months later, she told me: it was impossible to talk about what she had experienced there. Awe-struck she said: "There was no me anymore, not even my skin belonged to me ... a passage descended into the depths via four steps." She described a great letting go of things, without divulging any details. A forgiveness that had been "pure grace" and quite different from what she had ever done willingly, an "event." Then the black bowl reappeared, and she had given herself—no matter whether she died or remained alive—to God; an unspeakable peace had then come upon her. Returning to the here and now, Hildegard once again beheld the divided world. Watching this had been terrible, yet evil had not managed to harm her.—Weeks later she summed up what she had seen: a "completely different being, an utterly unintentional love." The path there led "through forgiveness." Everything was a "huge secret." She had returned with the task of living forgiveness day after day and yet knew no details; with whom, where or how. She would grow into this mystery.

Do reconciliation and forgiveness occur in freedom? When are we free anyway? My four-year-old nephew (see above) is definitely not free. But his parents, who are raising him and his sister between strictness and love, will offer him a good opportunity to grow into a mature and responsible person. Rahel may be able to forgive her father today, though not tomorrow. Time and again, she will find herself in the process of becoming conscious, between anger and generous forgiveness, with a general absolution granted to her father and to life—for her own and for love's sake. Time after time, she says "yes" to the process, demonstrating a wisdom of which only great personalities are capable. Initially, the words "my child" moved and softened her feelings.

Bassam Ramadani probably uttered the words "We forgive" partly of his own free will, partly he probably just spoke them along with his wife. But they did him good and entailed an all-encompassing "yes."

And Hildegard? She had not approached the subject deliberately. Instead, one day, what had been fermenting inside her for months had ripened and was imposed on her: she faced the appeal—freely yet humbly, listening for something greater. We might understand this as an impulse to mature from within—or as a call from something absolute. For Hildegard, her dreams and imagination came from depths she could not fathom.

1.2 What motivates us to engage in the process?

"The level of suffering" is probably the most frequent answer to this question. In earlier times, people might have said "So they are no longer short on domestic bliss," because they had learned "not to let the sun go down while you are still angry" (Ephesians 4:26). And because they assumed that love could be achieved in this way.

Today, we tend to think along different lines: "Forgive—for my own sake," and by doing so to free myself from a burden that I no longer wish to bear through life. We would like to actively decide to reflect on the positive and liberating resources of our life and to see our own history with fresh eyes. It is about wanting to live beyond bitterness and our own inner poisoning. The American physician Gerald G. Jampolsky titled his book on the subject *Forgiveness: The Greatest Healer of All* (1999). According to Jampolsky, those able to forgive with all their heart live healthier and happier lives.

Various motivations enable us to engage in processes of forgiveness and reconciliation, including that we wish to let go and make a fresh start. Love and spontaneity ought to flow freely again between us. Others do it for the sake of a child and its future. This motivation also enables them to better meet the challenge. One mother told me: "When I look at my boy, I no longer think primarily of myself. 'It' within me simply wants to do everything to make sure he's fine" (on the third person, see Sections 2.7 and 3.3).

Others, however, see another person's suffering and thus feel their own suffering relativized. Or they have a dream, a deep spiritual experience, for instance, during music-assisted relaxation or after an existential experience of being loved. Their spiritual experience opens the doors to the divine and awakens their desire for forgiveness and reconciliation (see the subcategories in phase 3, Section 3.3). Some people feel that their commitment to peaceful coexistence relates to the well-being of an entire community. Do we need people who stand up for a new togetherness? People who, by admitting their own inadequacy, are the first to interrupt the "blame game," a trading of accusations? What gives these people the strength? I assume that within us lies a deepest longing for salvation and connectedness, for a peace we are unable to create from within ourselves, yet which we can serve.

For example: I remember a simple 45-year-old woman, a mother of five children, who was married to an alcoholic ... She told me that when her husband attacked the children, she would stand in between,

18 *Why reconciliation? Why forgiveness?*

> *her arms outstretched (what a symbolic act!) and say: "You won't get passed me … if you have to hit someone, hit me … ." Aggressiveness should cease, she said, rather than be passed from one generation to another.*

This mother instinctively knew that law of human development according to which the suffering inflicted on a person—almost inevitably—turns evil in that former victim's soul: victims become perpetrators. And this hopeless cycle (on the perpetrator-victim cycle, see Stauss, 2010, p. 80 f.) must be interrupted.

1.3 Before major life transitions: The opportunity of being close to death

An urge for reconciliation is evident in particular before major changes in life. The reasons are manifold: we want to enter the new stage of life "at peace with ourselves" and untroubled by past burdens (e.g., after a divorce or career change). Or a new constellation emerges within a field of conflict: a mediator whom we can trust; the birth of a child; a health-related or some other existential change in one or the other conflict partner. Any such experience softens our hearts. Suddenly, there is a willingness to forgive, and a space of hope opens up. Or moving home or illness gives us more time to think about ourselves and everything.

Most of all, however, closeness to death makes us seek reconciliation and forgiveness. Writing about his wife's death, the theologian Dietmar Mieth observed: "Dying is a time of forgiveness. Love is a reason for forgiveness. Suffering an opportunity for forgiveness. Dwindling time is the driving force" (2019, p. 133). In our study, 42 out of 50 patients stated that their closeness to death impelled them to seek reconciliation and forgiveness. Expiring time urges us. The unresolved and the unredeemed pressure us deeply. Exhaustion relativizes resentment and makes forgiveness possible, which explains why it is sometimes referred to as exhaustion-induced forgiveness (Herzog, 2017, p. 23). Nevertheless, this applied only to one patient in our study. The rest were alert to the subject and some seemed to be waiting for reconciliation.

A longing for peace arises precisely near death. At work here are smoldering family conflicts, unresolved legal issues, the uncertainty about a child forever absent from one's deathbed, the burden of past wrongdoings or years of relentless noncommunication. In addition, there is a dynamic urge to resolve issues that often only have a chance

Why reconciliation? Why forgiveness? 19

of being looked at close to death. Widespread restraint—not wanting to impose anything on a dying person—faces inner necessity: often, life cannot be completed without finding the truth. During many years of attending to cancer patients and dying persons, I was called to many beds precisely because the dying could not die for some reason or another. When I gave lectures at hospice societies, many end-of-life carers reported similar observations. In our earlier study, "Dying is a Transition" (Renz et al., 2013; Renz, 2015), family processes were intensive and important.[1] Nevertheless, in the majority of cases, the dying no longer focused on their relatives at some stage,[2] probably due to shifting consciousness. The exception, however, were those dying patients who were deeply anxious about their children or plagued by family problems: they remained alert until the end and susceptible to the issue of reconciliation and forgiveness.[3] As if they were not free to die.

Conversations near death offer a great opportunity: the dying are increasingly immersed in a spiritual state, on the threshold to the greatest possible category change (from ego-existence to a state for which we have no words). The place where forgiveness and reconciliation succeed lies between two worlds, between the ego and God. This place is profane and holy, hopeless and healing. The dying see and hear differently and different things. Other things matter to them. They want to set a final focus in life, to find a personal legacy. They sometimes see more clearly what was bad in their lives, yet also the suffering they have silently helped bear and have endured for decades. Their own need for redemption becomes more palpable to them or confronts them on a symbolic level.

Forgiveness and reconciliation are as it were the final maturation step. The dying person no longer wishes to fall back into denial or rebellion. What is true, is unquestionably true. Forgiveness and reconciliation are the gateways to another world and atmosphere. The atmosphere around the dying—a holy earnestness—also changes relatives. They want to give the dying their utmost inner presence. Where fronts are still hardened and relationships subdued, it is sometimes my task as a therapist and spiritual caregiver to promote the process and to draw attention to what the situation demands.

> *During her illness, young Mrs Cadisch had been degraded for months by her teenage son and daughter. Now she was dying, yet neither child visited her. I was told that the mother was merely a heap of misery. I decided to talk to the children. What was the problem? I suggested that they should try to say goodbye in a way*

20 *Why reconciliation? Why forgiveness?*

that would still be good for them in a few years. I managed to talk to the family about the value and worthlessness of being sick and about empathizing a little with the sick. This gave both children some idea of how, with which sign of love, they could go to their mother's room. Mother and children met under new, dignified circumstances: the daughter gave her mother a warm scarf. The son said: "Mum, I don't understand you, but I couldn't endure what you can." Mrs Cadisch died a few days later.

Mr Nauer (a sarcoma sufferer about 50 years old) was assigned to me in the middle of a crisis. First contact (crisis).[4] *The next day, after music-assisted active imagination, Mr Nauer, who was religious only in the broadest sense of the word, told me about a spiritual experience he made when he had surgery a year ago: it was about a blue light, about love for the family and subsequently about a deep insight into guilt, even about his sense of having done wrong in matters of the heart. Something had been prised open. The illness and the hard-nosed business world had made him so hard-boiled that he had neglected his wife and children. Such was life (experience of hope). In spite of such estrangement from his family, this harsh man said that his deep relationships were helping him come to terms with his illness.*

In the following days, his symptoms escalated. Conflicts with his three adolescent children were in the air. His wife had given up on him emotionally: "He was just like that" (crisis). But he had found new hope. He was soft, as if something had fallen away from him when he entered the ward. Of course he loved his wife and children. He wept. She just shrugged her shoulders. I asked him directly: "Mr Nauer, do you love your wife?" He cried bitterly. This softened Mrs Nauer. She stroked him although a minute earlier she had believed that he was feigning his feelings. She asked why he never rang the children or sent them a text message. Sometimes he just needed a kick up the backside … He understood that she was scolding him and again assured her that he loved her. I took this as an opportunity to suggest that he (with my help) send each of his children a text message in the afternoon (experience of hope). While we were still together, the ward physician stepped into the room and was surprised to find that empathy, forgiveness, and decision had occurred.

In the afternoon, while I was still in the room, Mr Nauer took another decision: "Let us write three text messages."—"Dear Lara, I am fond of you. I understand that you are angry with me, but believe me, I love you. Kiss, Papa."—"Dear Veronique, my dear

Why reconciliation? Why forgiveness? 21

oldest daughter, you are sensitive, and our heart and soul. I love you, even if you are disappointed. Very much. Yours Papa."—"Dear Joel, I am so proud of you, even if I was often hard and silent. You are the greatest boy there is. I love you. Daddy." Mr Nauer writhed in pain, wheezed breathlessly, and wept so much writing every message that his mobile phone crashed several times because it had become soaked with tears. In the end, I wrote his dictated messages for him. He sent them, solemnly. As if his lips were praying. Mr Nauer was happy and relaxed for several hours.

The next day Mr Nauer's hope grew stronger. The older two children reacted sweetly. But the youngest, Lara, merely replied: "Ciao." Nevertheless, Mr Nauer sent everyone another text message, in even greater discomfort and weeping even more. He understood Lara. It hurt, but he understood. Once more he was happy after sending the messages (experience of hope). His wife visited and brought along photographs of their wedding day, exactly 20 years ago. They lay in each other's arms. She, too, was soft. Conscious reconciliation. Mr Nauer was expected to die quickly.

But not just yet. We waited five days. His wife would have liked to visit with the children, but they refused. My colleague and I offered support. The children came to see us, one at a time, each telling us briefly how they were doing. Lara said coolly that she did not care about anything. Dad didn't care about her, and she was done with such a person. Veronique said how much she was hurt. I explained that they were entitled to have their own feelings and could remain true to themselves. This would help to take the pressure off them, because Lara wouldn't soften if she felt obliged to. The two older children came with me to see their father. He wanted to make up with them (decision); he had never been so gentle. They all cried, sang, and prayed. I said a prayer of blessing. Mr Nauer said that Lara was among them in spirit. He understood her and let go of her, fictitiously. The oncologist, who had been treating Mr Nauer for many years, came in briefly. Deeply impressed, he said that he had never seen the patient so relaxed (reconciliation). Meanwhile, Lara was waiting in my office and soon returned home again.

Mr Nauer didn't die, contrary to all expectations. The next day he was calm, before growing restless again. The symptoms escalated (crisis). His wife, who had spent the night with him, was desperate. Why hadn't he been able to depart? I wondered whether he was waiting for Lara? He wasn't very responsive. I asked him, more

22   Why reconciliation? Why forgiveness?

emphatically, whether he was waiting until Lara had sorted herself out, until she could be with the rest of the family under happier omens when he died? "Yes." It was obviously not about him, but about his daughter. Again, he said "Yes" (experience of hope). His wife was impressed. But Lara still didn't want to come. She was, however, prepared to leave a message on his mobile phone, deeply moving words of farewell to her father. Amid escalating symptoms, he heard her words (reconciliation[5]), grew calm (after-effect), and died quietly 15 minutes later (after-effect[6]).

These examples illustrate that, as end-of-life carers, we also must take seriously the concerns, fears, and resistance of relatives. How much support do they need, and from whom? How long after death can they hold what they promised under the circumstances?

Nevertheless, I dare claim that closeness to death explains why so many dying persons ultimately go through their process to the point of reconciliation. In our study, almost all patients, 49 out of 50 (98%), experienced reconciliation or forgiveness, or both, at least once in the dying process, compared to 6 out of those 10 who did not die (60%). And 45 out of 50 (90%) were reconciled before dying, 4 in a state of denial, while one died after an experience of hope. Among those who did not die, however, 5 (50%) were in a state of reconciliation or forgiveness, or both, and 5 (50%) in a state of denial, before conflict and the need for reconciliation ceased being an issue for six months. They, too, knew that death was imminent (inclusion criterion), but things took a different course: these patients continued living.

Thus, in these cases, the closeness to death was not yet pressing. Thinking back to the many dying persons who have allowed me to participate in their process, I am convinced that while reconciliation and forgiveness may remain fragmentary, they nevertheless represent real and complete transformation. Like all dying, they happen into something ultimate, into God or the divine, from where transformation is perhaps also initiated. This is the great difference to reconciliation and forgiveness processes in the middle of life, where for most of us the dimension of the wholly other, non-dual, the divine is still far away. Dying happens at an outermost limit. It is a liminal experience par excellence—just as reconciliation and forgiveness seem to be. We need to conceive of reconciliation and forgiveness in terms of death, or in terms of spiritual connectedness, which seems to exceed or transcend us, and which occurs at the latest during our dying process. Take Mr. Nauer: connectedness meant nothing to him throughout his (professional) life. But illness and facing death led him to a deep connectedness, even to love.

1.4 Forgiveness and reconciliation as an expression of strength

Neither reconciliation nor forgiveness happens prematurely. Mahatma Gandhi is quoted as saying: "Weak people cannot forgive" (Stauss, 2010, p. 79). But what do they do? Lazily make peace, rashly and out of weakness? Or do they defer the conflict? Desmond Tutu (2014) aptly observed what forgiveness is not: it is neither easy nor passive; neither easily achievable nor a sign of weakness, nor a substitute for justice; nor to be confused with forgetting or repression (pp. 33–40). Andrea Herzog, a systemic therapist, religious educator, and healing practitioner (2017, p. 25), argues that in order to forgive we must remember what we want to forgive (see also Worthington, 2006; Worthington & Sandage, 2016; Section 2.9). Even if I cannot fully agree with this view—what about a dissociating torture victim,[7] what about the dying?—forgiveness includes at least some sense of what is involved, an emotional closeness to the subject. We let go of much hurt without needing to know any details.

Forgiveness and reconciliation mean that what was (as far as we can remember and feel) is still allowed to be true. We only find each other in truthfulness. Reconciliation and forgiveness cannot be demanded from outside. Or as the theologian and well-known psychotherapist Eugen Drewermann observed (1991, p. 145): "It is possible to say: 'I forgive you' if the pain doesn't burden us too much; because 'I forgive you' really only means: 'It wasn't that bad.' If, however, something has eaten itself deeply into our soul and pains us, honesty is more important than charity." When injuries no longer get in the way, wounds are "transfigured," and scars become symbols of strength.

Processes of reconciliation and forgiveness are about the truth. Usually, we must long endure tensions and unresolved issues. Suffering under such circumstances and struggling for reconciliation are signs of a strong personality—as is acknowledging that we do not simply embody the truth. Can we admit our own weaknesses? Are we able to quietly empathize with others, with a partner who keeps hurting us, or even with an erstwhile perpetrator? Is it conceivable that even their completely different view of the truth is not simply wrong? Such intuitions make us more human and bring us closer to ourselves, to our essence. We renounce power and prestige, discard a position of superiority and the armor of untouchability, and thus transcend the categories and patterns of our previous thinking. These are all signs of strength.

24 *Why reconciliation? Why forgiveness?*

Reconciliation and forgiveness grow from strength. But they also *guide* us towards strength and increase it—yet when exactly? And under which circumstances? While premature reconciliation and forgiveness weaken our psycho-physical system, because they demand something of us that we are not really capable of giving, when "their turn comes" (*kairos*), they lead to inner greatness and dignity. We are then at peace with ourselves; our actions are feasible and coherent. But why dignity, when we have been (and are still being) treated as worthless? If we do not need to hurt someone in return for the hurt we have suffered, but forgive them instead, we cease being victims. We will then have regained our dignity.

Considering this from the perpetrator's perspective leads to a similar result: if we are (literally) even willing to seek atonement, and thus willing to feel guilty, at least partly, we might feel ashamed, yet will have achieved something very difficult. This also becomes an experience of inner dignity. Only people with a strong character can do this. Shame is an individual concept. Neither the anonymous crowd is capable of shame nor those who hide behind it (Hell, 2018).

To repeat a basic question (Section 1.2): Why are reconciliation and forgiveness worthwhile despite considerable difficulties? The answer has many dimensions: reconciliation and forgiveness are liberating rather than aggravating. Something within us begins flowing, promising new hope and perspectives. We have to some extent left behind past burdens. We are temporarily released from patterns of repetition. We can complete a stage of life and embrace a new freedom and identity.

From the victim's perspective, we no longer give the other person—be they a perpetrator or simply a conflict party—power over our soul. From this perspective, Bishop Tutu (2014) regards forgiveness as *the* alternative to revenge. Significantly, he combines forgiveness with allowing ourselves to be reconnected (forgiving as reconnecting). He thus addresses the need for renewal on the relational level, leaving open *what* the relationship encompasses (connectedness with others, with ourselves, with God or with an ultimate existential basis; Section 1.6).

From the perpetrator's perspective, we achieve rehabilitation or reintegration through atonement—a new "innocence" or new "access to heaven," as one patient once impressively put it. Perpetrators are freed from a diffuse drivenness, from the pull of evil, which we need not elaborate any further (on evil, see Renz, 2020, Chapter 7).

1.5 What if the other side refuses?

But what happens if reconciliation remains one-sided? For instance, if the other person refuses, because they lack a sense of guilt and reconciliation, and perhaps "must" even persist to believe they have won? What then? Are we still able to achieve reconciliation, time and again? I believe that precisely then *forgiveness* becomes a form of self-inquiry. It, too, makes us free and uplifts us—nevertheless, we can only approach it cautiously.

What, however, if forgiveness is too great a challenge? Let me introduce the notion of futility in this respect. In German, forgiveness is even literally also about futility. By forgiving, the person who has been hurt, risks that much of their suffering was seemingly pointless: no one sees it, and there is neither jurisdiction nor rehabilitation. All too quickly, onlookers may blame us and distort the facts.

If we forgive nevertheless—and if this is not forced on us or altruistically demanded by others, but occurs because the time is ripe and we receive the necessary strength from within—then this strengthens our personality anew. *Inner* dignity takes the place of superficial appreciation. While perhaps we feared losing face, our personality grows. Reconciliation and forgiveness hinge largely on sincere willingness. Honesty, though, involves risk: ultimately, it remains open whether, even with a certain delay, or at some point, the other person sees reason and feels remorse in their own way. Even our friends often get left out; and also trained professionals, they are often unable to keep pace with a one-sided path to reconciliation. Reconciliation processes are subject to oscillate between denial or avoidance and willingness (see graphs, Appendix). Solutions are often "struggled for." Time and again, we risk forgiveness single-handedly—doing so is liberating (I discuss one-sided reconciliation more in-depth in Section 2.7).

1.6 Unreconciled conflicts affect us as relational beings

Guilt and forgiveness take effect beyond concrete action, beyond perpetrator or victim. Why? Because guilt threatens our fundamental connectedness, the inner flow of our vital and amorous energies. But forgiving—when forgiveness has occurred—restores connection and flow.

The physician and psychiatrist Konrad Stauss (2010) sees the following connections: as relational beings, we need this connectedness to live and love fully. In guilt, the perpetrator's relatedness is broken, and the same is true of the victim's hardened feelings. Our relatedness is

26 *Why reconciliation? Why forgiveness?*

constrained or even questioned. In such states, we are no longer connected to our deepest sources of life. Then begins a dynamics: it is as if the unreconciled person's feelings contaminate the atmosphere of entire families and groups even across generations. Consider, for example, Germany's process of coming to terms with the post-war guilt of its returning soldiers (unfortunately, this only happened in later generations) or the (merely gradually prevailing) insight that the traumatic memories of parents may persist unconsciously in children and grandchildren.[8]

Stauss (2010) had an Aha! experience when, in reflecting on forgiveness and reconciliation, he realized how much depends on our concept of humankind. If, following Darwin's theory of evolution, we believe that human beings are disposed solely to assert and preserve themselves, then forgiveness or reconciliation would not be an issue (or, it seems to me, only a marginal issue, for instance, serving to optimize group processes and communication). If, instead, we assume that we are relational beings, then forgiveness and reconciliation are hugely significant.

Stauss (2010) distinguishes three levels: the relationship with ourselves, the I-Thou relationship, and the relationship with the Eternal Thou. The first and second levels are self-evident. They concern forgiving ourselves and others, anyone with whom we are locked in conflict. Friedrich Nietzsche has Zarathustra say: "Ten times you must reconcile yourself with yourself; for overcoming is bitterness, and the unreconciled sleeps badly" (Nietzsche, 1883/2003, p. 20). But why, besides our relationship with ourselves, is our relationship with the Eternal Thou affected by the process of forgiveness?

Stauss (2010) has taught me above all that forgiveness does not occur in isolation. Whenever we ought to forgive someone, this also initiates a process within ourselves and towards a deeper existential basis. Our study confirmed Stauss's assumption: 38 out of 50 patients had conflicts with others, themselves as well as with God or fate (Figure 1, Appendix). Forgiveness often included a general "yes"—to everything.

The "Eternal Thou": the term itself implies that we are relational beings. We are related, since time immemorial and forever. We are an I that "has become" through its relationship with a Thou (Martin Buber) and which, through the Thou, finds itself more and more deeply and grows into relationships. I have even coined the phrase "The I dies into a Thou," which resonates profoundly with audiences whenever I use it as a lecture title. The dying themselves have taught me this: we seem to be deeply connected also in dying (Renz, 2015; Renz et al., 2018). Despite our presumed loneliness, we do not die

Why reconciliation? Why forgiveness? 27

withdrawn into ourselves: in death, we are not closed, yet open, in a transcendent relationship. This is an avowal of faith—and yet, it is also based on manifold observation and even experience: life and death seem to succeed when we are connected. Whenever I am part of a larger Whole, to which I belong, I feel nurtured and loved by it. Our primordial state is not one of self-sufficiency (autarchy), neutrality, isolation, or nothingness, but one of connectedness and openness. The same applies to an ultimate being, even if the whereupon remains open. Whenever our connectedness—or relatedness on whichever level (according to Stauss: the relationship with ourselves, the Thou, the Eternal Thou)—is disturbed, all levels are affected. Vice versa, forgiveness and reconciliation heal us on all levels. The dying say: "'it' flows again," "I feel a sense of meaning," "the circle has closed."

But why does departing from primordial connectedness have such momentous consequences? Why do we need redemption and forgiveness, if only to become more healed in our depths and more whole? Let me approach this question by offering an excursus about my model of the development of human consciousness. Linked to this is the question: What do we mean when we speak of sin?

Excursus: In the beginning was the Whole. The human ego did not develop out of nothing, from a tabula rasa, but rather out of belonging to the Whole. Becoming an ego went hand in hand with selection (in terms of brain physiology, the Whole is divided into particular aspects and interests, and the nascent ego is given the space to thrive as a center). As we develop, our perception changes. We perceive ever more from our own perspective, see the outside world accordingly, feel on our own terms, feel hungry as an ego … and react as an ego. This is a process. In the transition from being part of the Whole to becoming an ego, we experience fear for the first time as a rudimentary ego. This concerns existential fear: the fear of being completely lost in such tiny nothingness—while being threatened or flooded by the Whole, which we still perceive as numinous. If this experience of fear is pronounced, a tragic break with the Whole occurs, a separation (i.e., sin). As the ego and its position grow stronger, we lose our inner closeness with the Whole. The ego not only *detaches* itself from the Whole, but also loses its connection to it and the divine (e.g., the ability to perceive things differently, even the ability to perceive the Whole).

In human experience, this separation or sin was passed down from generation to generation as a code of human imprinting or as a behavioral pattern in the socialization process. The ancients vaguely intuited this and spoke of original sin. These events point to an almost inevitable factor in the development of human consciousness and the

28 *Why reconciliation? Why forgiveness?*

ego (Renz, 2017). The great church teacher Aurelius Augustinus, and later also the reformer Martin Luther, spoke of being encapsulated in oneself (*incurvatus in se*) (Tietz, 2005, p. 130). The term is interesting: encapsulated, we lose our connection to the divine and are no longer (equally) blessed and alive.

This excursus leaves me to conclude: forgiveness redeems us from separation and thus from splitting. Stauss, too, addresses the connection with the Eternal Thou (the Whole) in contemplating what might redeem us from being split, or even from sin. He highlights reconciliation and forgiveness because they overcome splitting! He also notes that in our world guilt—whether consciously or unconsciously—always involves a severing of our relationship with this Eternal Thou, and thus a state of sin. Forgiveness helps us reconnect, in every respect, also with the nurturing, invigorating, and healing fullness of life. Reconciliation, after all, acts as a gateway.

But how does forgiveness "function"? Stauss (2010) has developed a seven-step model of forgiveness.[9] While I cannot follow such a model in my depth-psychological and spiritually oriented work with cancer patients and the dying, I nevertheless sometimes recognize Strauss's three levels of relationship (with the I, the Thou, the Eternal Thou). Everyday clinical processes do not unfold schematically (see graphs, Appendix). Patients' symptoms and needs change from day to day, and our therapeutic measures and topics of conversation change accordingly. I am nevertheless grateful to Stauss that he also calls for our relationship with the Eternal Thou to be healed. My work as a music therapist offers even more possibilities to enable patients to experience the unspeakable: much of what is preconscious, and waiting for us to become conscious, resonates inconceivably in music and atmosphere. Even what is close to God, the divine, the spiritual, is already present in sound and vibration. Every dying person points out *their particular* way when they—sometimes through hard reconciliatory work—approach something that is perhaps intuited, heard, or even seen ... as an Eternal Thou.

The philosopher Hanna-Barbara Gerl-Falkovitz (2008, pp. 139–143) convincingly reflects on encompassing connectedness in terms of the history of religion. She argues that reconciliation and forgiveness developed as religion and culture emerged: monotheism became the *primordial space* in which the great rites of reconciliation arose. This development became possible in the intimate dialogue between the people and God. Here was the place where the Israelites could address and suffer under its infidelity. Accordingly, the longing for reconciliation was born here. In the threefold covenant (Noah, Abraham, Moses), the relationship between God and humankind is strong and at the same time capable of deep transformation: reconciliation no longer remains the sole responsibility of the law and the people, but—in the course of history—also becomes a matter of the heart and personal responsibility (Jer 31:33; Section 3.3). "On the one hand, the ego individualizes in being personally addressed by God ... , on the other hand, a We forms in the covenant theology of the chosen people" (Gerl-Falkowitz 2008, p. 139).

Notes

1 66 out of 80 patients in the pioneer project (=82%), 466 out of 600 in the follow-up project (=78%).
2 41 out of 80 patients in the pioneer project (=51%), 311 out of 600 in the follow-up project (=52%).
3 25 out of 80 patients in the pioneer project (=31%), 155 out of 600 in the follow-up project (=26%).
4 See also Renz et al. (2020), Forgiveness and reconciliation processes in dying patients with cancer: https://doi.org/10.1177/1049909119867675
5 This dot is barely visible on the graph (real time) because it is covered by the gray area representing the after-effect, which occurs so quickly that the two points in time are barely distinguishable.
6 We took corresponding notes whenever reconciliation took effect on the dying process.
7 Dissociation is a mechanism for coping with the almost unbearable, according to which a wrongful act is not only repressed in the aftermath but already split off during the wrongdoing as it were. Coming to terms with the past, those affected experience, all the terrible things as spiritually transfigured, for instance, surrounded by light. See Hermann (2015), Huber (2003), and Wirtz (2014).
8 See the insights of epigenetics into the consequences of physical and psychological traumas "inherited" over generations, for example, the tendency to premature births after the ancestors had suffered severe hunger due to warfare (see Lehnen et al., 2010; Steenwyk van et al., 2018).
9 According to Stauss, the seven steps of the forgiveness process are as follows:

1 Determining the traumatic key scene
2 Healing the relationship with ourselves
3 Healing the relationship with the Thou
4 Healing the relationship with the Eternal Thou
5 Performing a forgiveness ritual
6 Maintaining forgiveness
7 Reconciliation

Stauss also presents three variants of such relationship work: in the context of a therapeutic process, as an adult education topic, and as a spiritual exercise in the sense of a self-help guide (see pp. 123–125).

2 The need for perspective

2.1 Reconciliation and forgiveness happen after category change

As a rule, neither reconciliation nor forgiveness is self-evident. Both require certain inner and outer qualities. They proceed from a new perspective, one from which other things are seen or even perceived and considered differently. They happen when we cease "always having to be right," and when we cling to things, while allowing what once hurt so much to be true. Hannah Arendt (see 1958, p. 238) is credited with saying that "If we forgive, nothing will ever be the same again. Those who forgive become someone else—as do those who ask for forgiveness" (cited in Stauss, 2010, p. 78). This is what I mean by a category change: complete and previously inconceivable transformation. Where there was a caterpillar, there is now a butterfly. The most radical category change occurs when we die.

The New Testament describes reconciliation and forgiveness as "post-Easter processes." Through his message, Jesus introduced a fundamentally new and astonishing option into people's thinking and life: the kingdom of heaven is near (inside us, with us, in the here and now, wherever God is close). Jesus told us that when this option is present or in our hearts, even the unthinkable—that is, reconciliation and forgiveness—becomes possible. I am citing the Christian faith as an example here as it aptly illustrates the inherent law that hope precedes all reconciliation and forgiveness. In Christianity, the epitome of such hope is expressed in the belief in Jesus's resurrection. This, too, beautifully shows that forgiveness and reconciliation take place starting from a new state. According to the Gospel of John, Jesus demanded such processes, especially as the Risen One (John 20:23). Touched by the reality of the resurrection, the challenge of reconciliation and forgiveness was appropriate whereas those who

DOI: 10.4324/9781003310907-3

The need for perspective 31

gathered around Jesus during his lifetime did not understand these radical processes. Reconciliation and forgiveness were grasped in terms of Easter, after Jesus had offered all his vulnerability, and after transformation—from Good Friday through Holy Saturday to Easter—had occurred in the souls of those around him.

Below I explore various aspects of such transformation and under which conditions it occurs:

Spaces of feeling (Section 2.2)

Conscious realization, post-maturation, truth-finding (Section 2.3)

A new empathy (Section 2.4)

Renunciation, waiting, trusting (Section 2.5)

With the help of a third party (Section 2.7)

Risking vulnerability or the significance of scapegoats (Section 2.8).

Each individual case requires considering two perspectives: What do victims need? What do perpetrators need? These questions concern not only those who have become either victims or perpetrators but also the victim or perpetrator aspect in all of us (Sections 2.9 and 2.10). There are many paths and models of reconciliation—spiritual, therapeutic, and ritualistic (Sections 2.11 and 2.12)—some of which I discuss below.

Let me begin with an insight that pervades my life and its challenges as a basic conviction: *we need perspective*. In the middle of life and, invisibly, even before death. Reconciliation and forgiveness pre-suppose, yet also create experiences of happiness. The more serious suffering was and is, the more important perspective and happiness are. But why happiness? I am indeed speaking of happiness, grace, and experiences of hope. At some point, many sufferers need to approach life differently in search of that fullness, love, as well as earthly and supernatural sustenance from which they can overcome past hurt day after day. In my therapeutic work, and in supporting those hit hard by fate, I keep starting out in this direction time and again. At the same time, I know that all of us, including myself, lag behind in seeking to overcome suffering: we are sometimes happy and yet often, perhaps even every day, also desperate.

How can people who have suffered profound hurt go on living? How can they stay alive? This is an important question in the process of forgiveness and reconciliation. Can they, can we *want* forgiveness even when salvation is not realistic or intangible? I believe we

32 *The need for perspective*

can—time and again—if peace or grace just happens. This *Kairos* is liberating—each and every time.

2.2 Spaces of feeling

Reconciliation and forgiveness become possible when hurt, violation, and admissions of guilt fall into caring, circumspect hands. They mature when a neutral third party feels with us and values us as we go through our process. When the injured person dares to increasingly feel their hurt and when the guilty endure their guilt as being true. I thus ask

- Where are those spaces in which what happened is allowed to be true and where mourning is allowed and also given time to be overcome?
- Where is a counterpart who accepts difficult feelings?
- Where are those who empathize and think with us? Those mothers and fathers whose forgiving love sets an example to their children and thus that forgiveness is worth the effort.
- Where are those communities that find togetherness in their struggle for hope, endure processes, and still celebrate the corresponding rites?
- Where is that God who is still God, who empowers, graces, and mercifully embraces us, and whom we still experience as such?

2.3 Conscious realization, post-maturation, truth-finding

Reconciliation and forgiveness involve conscious realization, tenacious effort to achieve consciousness. They happen if we say "yes" to the process and wish to engage in it, day after day. And if we wish to become conscious and take steps towards finding the truth. Not without good reason have pioneering authors like Robert D. Enright, Everett L. Worthington, Desmond Tutu, Frederike von Tiedemann, Konrad Stauss, and Melanie Wolfers highlighted a fundamental point: *forgiveness is decision.* As a rule, one does not go back on a decision. It is precise because reconciliation and forgiveness are so difficult that temptations such as procrastination or prematurely cutting off the process are bound to arise. And yet, can we resist these temptations?

Becoming conscious and finding the truth are laborious and painful processes. Considering our own shadow to be true is shameful. And it is anything but easy to recognize our own projection in the images we

The need for perspective 33

create of the "enemy": "He always needs to be right," we often say reproachfully when having the last word matters to us. Power and the greed for power are almost always involved. And barely anything is more difficult than recognizing how comprehensively our everyday thinking and acting are determined by the greed for power, violence, and prestige. These reactions are internalized like reflexes. Others, in particular slow processes such as becoming mindful and mature, but also an awareness of injustice, have developed only rudimentarily in our culture. And yet, repentance and purification would require precisely such slow processes.

Would it be better if we returned to the idea of the guilt-ridden human being, guilty solely because he or she exists, and who—symbolically speaking—has eaten from the tree of knowledge? The question is futile. Moreover, such a concept of humankind is not suited to achieve true reconciliation—either with ourselves, or with others, or with life. It makes us submissive, yet not inwardly free. It would simply prevent the goal of religious development in Judaism and Christianity: to consciously face (and answer to) God or an outermost Thou. Such a disposition and goal of the biblical religions becomes rudimentarily apparent already in the Book of Genesis, where there is mention of "being in the image." Jews and Christians in particular hear the prophet Jeremiah articulate this idea when he presents the vision of peace and a new covenant:

> But this will be the covenant that I will make with the house of Israel after those days … I will put my law within them, and I will write it on their hearts … No longer shall they teach one another … for they shall all know me, from the least of them to the greatest … for I will forgive their inuity, and remember their sin no more (Jeremiah 31:31–34; restated in Hebrews 8:8–12).

It is unfortunate that for centuries the monotheistic religions and the cultures to emerge from them have one-sidedly adopted the perpetrator's perspective and have focused chiefly on the guilty and the victors. Little, however, has been handed down in the Judeo-Christian religious tradition about victims' wounds (as advocated by liberation theology, for example) (Section 2.9).[1] Just as sparse is contemplating the possibilities for developing *beyond* the categories of right versus wrong, victory versus defeat. But how might we overcome such a one-sided orientation towards power and perpetrator? What makes love and peace possible?

Once more, the notion of a category change occurs to me: a transition, a new way of thinking … Buddhism, for instance, teaches us to

34 *The need for perspective*

stop thinking in terms of guilt, that is, causal thinking per se. Doing so introduces an atmosphere of greater being, mindfulness, and deceleration. And yet, in the West, this remains but a limited answer both to the hurt inflicted and to what we have become.

In our culture, the human being is geared towards development, individuation,[2] and personal relationships. In themselves, these guidelines would actually lead to responsible living. The relationship is crucial in this respect. Many people have been irritated, hurt, or debased precisely as relational beings (by individuals, by collectively rooted patterns of exercising power). And they have subsequently encapsulated themselves and become untouchable (narcissistically, for instance). How can they allow their depths to be touched ever again? Mindfulness and meditation alone are not enough in the face of this relational challenge. For relational challenges, we need relational experiences. The path to such experience involves awareness and post-maturation, probing and suffering, feeling and waiting.

Truth-finding happens mentally, emotionally, and through body-work. It includes working on ourselves, on relationships, and on community structures (Tutu 2014). The ability to be touched, new relational patterns, and collective regulations mature slowly. All too quickly do we ignore another person's coming to consciousness—and yet this process cannot be cut short in the long run. South Africa's Truth Commission is merely one example in contemporary history. Others include the history of the Christian church or Jesus's legacy. We need repetition in order to become ever more conscious. We need both the pioneer *and* painstaking attention to detail in everyday life; suitable paths lead via the first *and* the second generation, or even via the third. And perhaps also via the third millennium and resurgent hope.

On this path, and the work it involves, we Westerners are helped chiefly by new *relational experiences*: a deeper, truer sense of understanding and being loved (e.g., by our partner, therapist, or spiritual/pastoral carer). Healing also comes from positively charged philosophical or religious answers to our ultimate longing. Sometimes this also finds expression in dreams.

> *One woman dreamed, "You are important in the garden of God," and saw herself weeding there. What she experienced in this dream enabled her to experience dignity.*

Are reconciliation and forgiveness meaningful? Do they help us to embark on such spiritual paths? I believe so—precisely because they concern the relational level. Without lived forgiveness, we are almost

The need for perspective   35

never able to overcome binary thinking (in terms of polar opposites) or the need to be right all the time. Unless we live forgiveness, we will never achieve a life of fulfilled (and not altruistically selfless) devotion. The goal of such maturation is to find a new identity, freedom, and love. Nevertheless, the question remains whether forgiveness needs to occur explicitly and with the necessary awareness, also with regard to the dying.

2.4 Reconciliation and forgiveness begin with new empathy

Whenever we manage to empathize and feel, however fragmentarily, from another's perspective, forgiveness becomes possible—and reconciliation is afforded the genuine opportunity.

The wars of the last century at the very latest highlighted the fact that the horror inflicted on one generation lives on in later generations. It has consequences, takes explicit or unconscious effect, and is unconsciously restaged in future generations. Certain issues run in families: alcohol, depression, brutality, incest, suicide. The repetitions may feel like a curse—and yet they enable us to understand the difficult word "curse" as a phenomenon. Mr. Camenisch's story illustrates this point:

> *Mr Camenisch, a small, fine-boned man, was sitting upright and fully dressed on his chair—his unopened suitcase next to him. He had been admitted the day before. The bed was untouched. He told me that he had spent the night in the armchair. This touched me. We greeted and he said that he had always struggled with depression. He was receiving the right medication, but ... everything was pointless. He was divorced, lived alone and rarely had visits from his daughter, whom he and his wife had adopted at the time, as her frigidity had made a sexual relationship impossible. Frustrated and because of the family difficulties, he had drunk too much ... and had always been out of sorts ... for as long as he could remember. The extent of his forlornness shocked me. He did not feel at home, neither inside the hospital, nor outside ... What did him good, I asked. "Deep relationships, which sounds absurd, I know, because there is nobody there ... I love animals ... the forest. In the forest behind my house I sometimes feel a closeness." But he was unable to interpret this feeling spiritually. Religion and spirituality were illusions, he exclaimed!—How strange, because this man's gaze felt cultivated and sensitive, his words differentiated, his gestures subtle. But he easily became cynical (see denial).*

36 *The need for perspective*

Mr Camenisch was going to have an operation and had to change wards. When I visited him, he was pleased but cynical. If things turned worse, he would opt for assisted suicide. He was a lost cause anyway (denial). The next day I visited him again. He was pleased. He liked me and enjoyed telling me about his life. After a while, he told me that the conflict with his brother and his family persisted. But he didn't want to have anything to do with them at the moment. "Death … " He faltered and fell silent. I asked if he wanted to know about my experiences with the dying? "Yes!" His daughter came into the room and listened too … What I told them about palliative medicine and about experiencing a condition beyond symptoms gave them a sense of hope. I still didn't really know why this was so important for Mr Camenisch. I asked him. He said that everyone in his family had committed suicide. As if they were cursed. But now he had heard about my observations with so many dying people, and this gave him "an alternative." Assisted suicide would nevertheless remain an option. However … . The next day, he was cynical again and wanted his peace and quiet (denial). Three days later, he grew restless. His symptoms and his wish to commit suicide increased (crisis). This condition persisted even four days later; dissatisfaction and irreconcilability (with people, with himself, with God, with everything …) were plainly evident, yet remained unaddressed (crisis); in fact they became prevalent.—Mr Camenisch's issues preoccupied me. Who felt responsible for him? Who liked him? The next day, I visited him once again. I felt compassion for him. My presence, our conversations and the prospect of soon returning home brightened his mood (experience of hope).

Mr Camenisch was readmitted almost three weeks later, this time to the palliative ward. Hope had persisted, he reported. Care also gave him a sense of esteem (experience of hope). Three days later: he was still hoping, and cried for the first time. The nurse interpreted this as him making new contact with his own feelings (experience of hope). After another three days, he felt "heard" by me as a therapist. The conversations with me were "honest and touching." He felt understood and was surprised that someone like him could be understood at all. I recalled our initial conversation and his desire for deep relationships … (experience of hope). But already by the evening he was once again trapped in restlessness, despair and his symptoms. The desire to commit suicide and his feelings of being cursed were omnipresent, even if they were never broached (crisis). I went home empty-handed and asked myself whether an urge lay behind

The need for perspective   37

Mr Camenisch's repeated setbacks ... The next day, his brother's wife called me.

The family's cursed history now became more tangible for me. I visited Mr Camenisch again and asked him directly: "Dear Mr. Camenisch, what is on your mind? Do you need reconciliation? You know, I like you, you're a cultivated person. Your brother's wife called me. This has given me a better sense of your hopelessness ... it is like a shadow story ... it comes from the left and from the right and there is barely a way out." "What? Is anyone meant to understand this? ... are you and even she (i.e., his brother's wife) interested in me?" Mr Camenisch smiled and held my hand (experience of hope).

The next day, he was—at long last—ready. He told me about his family and about connections that were no longer clear to him ... ; he told me about his grandfather's suicide in the stable, about the overshadowed Christmas party ... he decided that "now or never" he wanted to speak to his brother and his family in his daughter's presence and mine as a therapist. And: he did NOT want to commit suicide, even if everyone in his family had. He wanted to tell everyone (decision). The conversation took place three hours later. Almost solemnly, Mr Camenisch told his brother and his wife about his decision. She cried, his (adopted) daughter was impressed and said that her father's resolve also provided her with a new way out, after she had previously only regarded suicide as an option for herself: "The outcome is now open!" I paid tribute to father, daughter and the family, but pointed out that Mr Camenisch's brother, who still wanted to end his life with assisted suicide, remained free to decide for himself. Freedom was the word for everyone. Mr Camenisch emphasized that he would follow the palliative route (reconciliation). At 6 a.m. the following morning, the night nurse reported that relaxation had continued during the night (after-effect), and that medication had remained stable. Three hours later, Mr Camenisch became somnolent (after-effect). He died shortly after lunchtime.

Mr. Camenisch is one of many patients who are overshadowed by family issues. Other patients speak of depression and addiction, compulsive adultery, white-collar crime, and domestic abuse. The spiral of inescapability opens up via empathy, sometimes expressed by the conflict party, often by neutral third parties.

38   *The need for perspective*

Certain themes also recur collectively, within entire ethnic groups or cultures: violence and oppression, a striking proclivity for suicide in a region, persecution and war, addiction, and lethargy. Some issues affect our entire planet, such as the lost feeling for nature. Guilt is always involved, directly or indirectly. How, though, can this guilt complex be reverted? It is a question of human fate whether later generations are prepared to become conscious of guilt and its consequences and to engage in reconciliation work. This includes clarifying, differentiating, feeling, mourning, affirming, putting into context and perspective—in an empathetic atmosphere. What happened in the past will be understood and reappraised.

In recent decades, the realization has grown that reconciliation processes are necessary—in the public and in the private sphere. We have developed corresponding sources of help: besides expert political and economic conflict resolution, professional fields such as mediation, family counseling, ombudsmanship, peace work in schools, and couples coaching (von Tiedemann, 2017) have emerged. These all rely on empathy among conflict partners (see also Worthington 2006 and Section 2.11). Why did the other person behave as they did, and not differently? Is it possible to gain insight into their emotional state and motivation, body tension, emotional baggage, and formative influences? In therapy sessions, I often fictitiously bring the absent person into the room and conduct a targeted empathy exercise. Here are some possible answers or reactions to this exercise:

> *An older woman described her husband's state of mind as follows: "Everything is so leaden. His body and feelings are so stunted that he can impossibly feel anything for his wife."*

> *A newly retired man now had time for his wife but she rejected him. The empathy exercise helped him understand: "I would never have thought that my wife is so burdened by the past. Now I understand that she's always depressed."—This man wanted to help his wife rid herself of the old burden and to gain a sense and deeper feeling of herself. He asked her about her parents: How had she grown up? What were their values? What was forbidden at home? What did the children laugh and quarrel about? Pondering these questions conjured up a previously unknown image of his wife's childhood, which in turn changed his behaviour towards her.*

> *A young woman, who wanted to better understand her partner with this exercise, said astonished: "In his position, I feel an incision running through me from top to bottom: above, decisions are made*

and action taken. Below lies frozen anger." The empathy exercise helped her to appreciate her husband, even if he held back his feelings. This in turn astonished him positively.

The exercise is simple and involves changing perspective: two chairs are placed in a room, one for the client, the other for a person whom the client experiences as difficult or even hostile. Clients always begin with themselves, first sensing their own questions and addressing these to the fictitious counterpart (i.e., towards the other chair). Next, they change chairs and are asked to feel what comes towards them from the other side. How does what is said feel in this position? How does sitting on this chair feel physically, in terms of breathing and muscle tone? Do they feel resistance? Does any unexpressed fear lie behind this position? Which words of love would be encouraging?

After feeling their way into their counterpart, clients can try out a dialogue: they articulate what they would like to tell the other person, for instance: "I love you" or "I realize that I shouldn't get too close to you with my questions." The dialogue is refined as we move back and forth between first-person ("I") messages and tracing our feelings. This allows clients to experiment with a new form of behavior in a (sheltered) therapy setting.

2.5 Renunciation, waiting, trusting: Overcoming hard times

In our project, we did not refer to "renunciation." This keyword was not a point on the path towards reconciliation, and thus nothing to be ticked on the observation sheet. We (the members of our study team) found this word too delicate and felt that physicians, nurses, therapists, and even spiritual carers would misunderstand it—as it seemed suspect and outdated. But is this true?

Fortunately, belief in the devil as personified evil is fading. But the knowledge of the ancient desert fathers, who were able to cope with barren times, outwardly and inwardly, remains explosive. Lean periods still shape maturation processes today. They sometimes call for reconciliation and forgiveness and need to be endured: it is often a matter of waiting almost interminably while not succumbing to temptations such as distraction, consumerism, self-disparagement, and addiction.

Whom or what must we moderns renounce? The temptations are manifold. We are especially fragile when hurt or threatened and must refute impulses for revenge, self-pity, resignation, or theatrical profit-making. We need a mature, conscious approach to anger and fear.

40 *The need for perspective*

Anger "exists," as does fear. Our body and soul are affected even before we realize what is at stake. Unresolved conflicts or even guilt pressure us. Old wounds fester whenever they were unable to heal once inflicted.

We are haunted by anger and fear especially at night, the real and inner dark times of life. This is what the image of the desert stands for: the spiritual test is greatest whenever the most existential necessities are lacking—also when we feel forlorn and misunderstood.

Who takes charge? Realizing that leadership is needed at all is itself a humble insight. Without leadership, we are at the mercy of ourselves, of our temptations or whims. We would need a compass or a guide dog, something that points us towards the next step: forwards, backwards, sideways, standing still. The desert fathers were guided by their closeness to God and by intuition. The mystic recognizes guidance even in God's absence. He has the grace to also interpret mystical darkness religiously and to trust himself in its midst. What, however, helps the elderly pensioner, what the seriously ill patient during her long nights? What helps amid pain? What amid profound anxiety?

> *Mr Benedetti, a 29-year-old leukaemia patient, confessed: "I must be able to call my wife also at midnight. If I can't, I listen to the same piece of music all the time, think of my cat, and cuddle a teddy bear instead ... everything is about trust. Then the night is won."*

Trust is *the* crucial word and also means "to renounce fear." I often recommend patients to say a short nocturnal prayer, one which I also take to heart and practise myself: "I trust." Or: "God, I trust." It is first of all an expression of will, second a mantra that at the same time becomes a structure-creating rhythm, and third a (spiritual) activity. And, as I practise, something happens ...

2.6 How realistic is reconciliation as a mutual process?

When we speak of forgiveness, as a rule we mean present conflicts, ones we can put our finger on family problems, couple conflicts, reappraising conflicts politically or legally after years of warfare. Without saying so explicitly, we assume that reconciliation occurs mutually. In her groundbreaking book on reconciliation in couples therapy (2017), the psychotherapist and supervisor Frederike von Tiedemann describes a series of practical steps (see pp. 82–153), in a setting where a helping third person (therapist) supports the partner locked in conflict. Let me formulate some of these practical steps in my own words:

The need for perspective 41

- drawing up a framework agreement
- recognizing conflict patterns, interrupting destructive interactions, turning reproaches into wishes
- fostering a positive atmosphere of dialogue and reciprocity, recognizing the resources of a shared history
- seeing the relationship through the other person's eyes
- making visible past or present wounds that have remained open
- taking account and, in so doing, distinguishing between intention and effect
- taking responsibility for hurtful behavior, asking for forgiveness, and forgiving; the phrase "I'm sorry" is important in this respect (p. 146).

von Tiedemann distinguishes injuries—mostly single actions—that can be brought to a close through a process of forgiveness and reconciliation from those whose impact continues to affect us and is felt every day (p. 149). The latter include recurring hurt, for instance, a woman who repeatedly committed adultery. Although she was sincerely sorry, she cheated on her husband again. Under such circumstances, as von Tiedemann explains, "the gesture of forgiveness loses its effect" (p. 192). The woman's need for "affirmation is stronger than her self-control" (p. 192). In my experience, unconscious backgrounds often lead to periodically or even constantly repeating the same behavior.

I remember one patient who, as his wife told me, lambasted her every three weeks. I asked this man whether "anything in your childhood had lasted three weeks?" He had grown up in former Eastern Germany and spontaneously replied: "As a boy, I was detained for exactly three weeks in a concentration camp for children. There was nothing my parents could do."

I often observe that constantly recurring hurtful behavior is, as it were, part of a person's not understood personality or unconscious character. It concerns their own childhood and formative influences. And then what?

The psychotherapist and theologian Norbert Wilbertz (2017, p. 205) has remarked that with many couples the process of reconciliation falters when everyday interactions "are linked to childhood hurt and when barely or inadequally healed wounds re-open ... ." The severity of reactions is not comprehensible. Von Tiedemann adds: relationships are "finite" (p. 192). If one person's "wrongdoing far exceeds what another person can cope with and come to terms with, or if the hurtful

42 *The need for perspective*

behaviour even transcends our cultural framework because it involves physical superiority or even violence, then the limits of reconciliation have been reached" (p. 192).

There are obviously limits to the resilience of relationships. Nevertheless, I regret—without wishing to judge individual cases—how quickly separation and divorce often occur. It seems that it is not enough to refer couples to depth psychology when one's family of origin or related issues become important. These topics also need to be integrated into couples therapy. In over 20 years of psycho-oncological work, I have also counseled the relatives of several hundred patients. What I initially understood only approximately, based on exemplary marriage dynamics (see Mrs Brunner's case in Renz, 2017, p. 151 f), I now recognize as a *rule*:

> Relationship conflicts touch on childhood experiences. Especially when reconciliation processes are one-sided (which is usually the case), and when the motivation to engage in these processes is one-sided, couples need help from a third party. And they need motivating experiences of hope. These come from outside or from deep inside and are experienced as grace.

2.7 Third parties enable reconciliation and forgiveness

Whenever childhood hurt is stirred, this often concerns what must first be grasped in words and felt. It also concerns behavioral patterns, which affect not only individuals but possibly several generations or entire clans. When I think of victims and perpetrators, the guilty may have died long ago; they, too, were not only perpetrators but also victims. Or as a dying father most remorsefully confessed to the daughter he had abused: "It was just like that ... everyone in our village did it." Severe childhood hurt is often tabooed.

How, or with whom, should we seek reconciliation? Whom do we forgive or accuse? Are such processes possible and feasible when nobody hears us – into emptiness? Working at deathbeds has taught me that these processes are sometimes necessary—and fate-changing—in order for us to die. Not only closeness to death, but already serious illnesses beforehand move us towards forgiveness and reconciliation. And this requires concrete help.

> *Mrs Halter was confused and unsure. How should she respond to her brother's accusation? She was unable to comment. Experience told me that it was important not to probe deeper in such moments.*

The need for perspective 43

Mrs Halter trembled and asked herself: "Why am I so disturbed and vulnerable?" She often felt like this, she said—as if she lost sight of the facts. Was this perhaps due to her cancer? Mrs Halter had metastatic bowel cancer. The diagnosis had upset her profoundly. Old issues had been reactivated. I managed to reassure her that this was normal. She responded well to body perception exercises and felt both confused and clear-sighted. Feeling helped ground her. Then she told me with amazing clarity: she had seen her brother again for the first time in many years. This had been good at first and yet too much. He accused her of severing contact with their father. "If only he knew ... ," she told me. After the meeting, Mrs Halter also distanced herself from her brother. She now suffered from nightmares and fits of rage again. Her sister was dead. Mrs Halter had grown up with foster parents. Her biological father had drunk, beaten her, and sexually abused her sister. Mrs Halter was still trembling. She was "deeply upset" and confused. I praised her for enduring this state of mind and for sharing her thoughts and thus also herself. Her imprinting and concrete experience with her brother explained the nightmares, the anger attacks, as well as her confusion. It took weeks for Mrs Halter to feel grounded again.

Then, she asked me what she should do about her children? Neither her daughter nor her son barely knew anything about her childhood—and she didn't feel able to tell them. We prepared a family meeting between mother and children, in which I would speak on Mrs Halter's behalf. We met and the children were grateful to hear their mother's story. It explained quite a bit, they said. They, too, were full of incomprehensible fear, anger, and self-aggression— as if something had been silently transferred onto them.

This meeting was merely a beginning. It probably succeeded not least because, as a neutral third person, I intervened as soon as the slightest accusation arose and explained to the other party that this, too, was normal (e.g., the mother's confused state of mind or the daughter's self-aggression). They (mother, daughter, son) wished to meet again a few weeks later. I asked them, quite directively, not to discuss the matter in the meantime. They understood that such conversations need a sheltered space, as well as an appreciative third person who puts matters in perspective and interrupts if necessary. And that the process needed time precisely because "it" was so bad.

Third parties enable that space of trust in which we can find words and grow aware—even when our conflict parties are absent (Mrs. Halter's

44   *The need for perspective*

parents had died, and her brother was not present during her conversations with me). Reconciliation processes—as in this example of coming to terms with the past—need a sheltered space. An impartial person carefully protects the vulnerable person from being overwhelmed by conflict, confrontation, and outside reactions. The third party is a guarantor. He or she can be trusted. Concretely, this may be a friend, a pastor, a therapist, a lawyer, or ultimately even God or the Supreme Being. An ally! For Gerl-Falkowitz (2008), following the philosopher Jacques Derrida (2001), "the third" always refers to the absolute. To forgive the inexcusable is only possible from the viewpoint of the absolute (p. 194 f). I use the term of "the third" more openly: either another person or God himself/the Supreme Being may be a third party, serving as an inner source or point of reference. The absolute is a time-independent giver and takes effect in the individual. Forgiving the unforgivable also happens through many manageable instances of forgiving.

In our study, "the third party" proved decisive in 43 out of 50 patients. Whenever appropriate predefined subcategories within the experience of hope and decision (see endnote) were ticked, this was counted.[3] I speak of a third party whenever a patient experiences another person or God himself/the Supreme Being as motivating, clarifying, structuring, or establishing justice. The third party, for instance, encourages making contact, provides resonance, and creates space for creative solutions, which often lead the way out of and beyond preprogrammed repetition. Or the third party is what simply loves:

Job's Female Companion

You—are my lover,
I—am your beloved. Am I?
I will not sit here for seven days and nights
in silence beside you.

You—assailed by suffering—
do *not* want to be Job. Are you?
Day after day you sink into namelessness, have long given up
yourself and God.

Aye, I will lie on the floor next to your bed.
Can I reach you?—The floor is cold.
You just ask, "What are you doing?"
At night, a scream—you have *never* screamed before.

The need for perspective 45

And I know: If I can "hold" your soul,
then you *are* held, leaving you be and carrying you.
—Help, I can *not* do any more than I can!
I can.

Monika Renz, December 2016 (first published in Renz, 2017).

2.8 Risking vulnerability: The significance of scapegoating

Reconciliation processes are often one-sided. For instance, when the other person has died or does not want reconciliation (Section 1.5). Only mature persons are willing to accept and approach a conflict as a unilateral process. In our study, 13 patients risked such a heroic path. Twelve of them eventually experienced an encounter with the adversary or the other side under new auspices. I attribute this frequency to the proximity to death. The 13th patient remained alone until her death and emanated deep peace: she had become *internally* reconciled.

How can unilateral reconciliation processes be described? How do they work?

Mrs Tuner was referred to me by the nursing staff with the hint that she kept being humiliated by her husband and didn't know how to cope. The doctor saw this differently, claiming that Mrs Tuner was a neurotic victim.—Now, a frightened, cautious, finely boned, and differentiated woman stood outside the door and knocked so quietly that I couldn't hear her. One of our first issues was that she was entitled to make her presence felt. The figure of an angel in my therapy room caught her attention. Mrs Tuner prayed a lot, yet she said that she neither knew who God was nor whether he helped. She talked about her marriage, about her husband's reactions, who not only belittled her every day, but had already hit her. Then, sometimes, she lost her voice, was unable to express and defend herself. Now, Mrs Tuner turned away abruptly before continuing, in a strikingly different tone, that she was probably to blame for everything. I firmly rejected this, adding that her story impressed me and that some people scapegoated their partner. Mrs Tuner looked at me surprised. Really? So she was normal after all? Well, perhaps not normal, but credible?

Our sessions helped her increasingly find her voice, and she began to believe herself. Her husband, a successful dentist had become ill-tempered since his retirement and abused her verbally every day. For

46 *The need for perspective*

years, he considered it unnecessary to finish refurbishing their kitchen. They had to live with the scaffolding. She didn't know why she put up with things, and yet she was still there. Once she went to Ireland for three months, which was good, but not right. And thus, she continued to stay with him—but why? Once more, my role was to normalize matters: even one-sided love and marriage could be absolutely right. Mrs Tuner began contemplating the reasons for her marriage and for staying with her husband: when she was young, her husband had given her security; his physical presence alone had done her good and had led her away from the atmosphere back home to herself. The Tuners had had three children, who now mocked her. She stayed with her husband because he was ill (although less than her) and because this was her home. Body perception exercises, music-assisted relaxation, and imagination strengthened and animated Mrs Tuner. On several occasions, she saw herself as "a woman honoured by God." What could this mean?

Mrs Tuner needed therapy as a sheltered space of feeling. She needed me to appreciate her, to end her self-deprecation, and to put matters into context. Above all, God began mattering to her. She recovered quite quickly and managed—as if nurtured by God—to take herself sufficiently seriously and to defend herself. She created a space of her own in her house and garden, to which she retreated to collect her thoughts and pray every day. She now valued herself, and so did her children. Her husband now respected her at least. For months, Mrs Tuner blossomed again.

Although Mrs Tuner was not explicitly concerned with reconciliation, she lived it constantly, daily. When I asked her about this, she confirmed that she had to forgive her husband, herself, life, and even God time and again. She wanted to understand the concept of the therapeutic third party: What exactly had helped her? And how could she implement this on her own? How could the intangible, remote God help her even if she still needed to be loved by a real person?

One day, Mrs Tuner came for therapy and summed up matters: there was something like an incomprehensible motivation to stay in love. This idea interested me, and I asked her to say a bit more. What was this motivation? Shrugging her shoulders, she replied: "In love itself. I can't understand it, but I'm happy to love. I'm happy in my places, inside and outside. I recharge my energies there and wish for a better world. Can that alone be motivation?"

She discovered Jesus, who also loved, incomprehensibly, out of an inner source, even more than she did. She had recently dreamed of Jesus: he was lying there, immensely charismatic. But she felt confused because his face resembled hers. He had put a vast house and garden in order, had brought the house to life and had planted the garden. The dream gave her utmost inner dignity.

Mrs. Tuner strengthened my conviction that unilateral reconciliation is possible. She taught me so much about life:

- Despite all the one-sidedness in her life, she found places of strength and trust for herself.
- She had found Jesus ... who had somehow become identical with her (note: not *she* became identical with him, because this would be megalomania, but *he* came to her).
- She rediscovered herself and her strength—an amazing transformation.
- Outwardly, she was compelled to move forward alone—and often took suffering on herself without resisting. In an inner perspective, she felt like a sacrificial lamb; for her husband (from an outer perspective), she was a scapegoat. That is not the same.
- Meanwhile, not much happened on her husband's side that would have changed their relationship. Some fellow therapists whom I discussed this case with believed that the husband probably saw matters differently. Perhaps! To him, as he told the oncologist and me, psychological processes were pointless. His contempt was perhaps a projection of his own inferiority, for which his wife had long been a thankful object. Yet no longer.
- Mrs. Tuner is certainly an outstanding example. But perhaps her story reveals a reality that sometimes occurs on either a larger or a smaller scale: a relationship that continued because this woman endured it. Nevertheless, I did not consider Mrs. Tuner to be a masochist—after all, she loved her "sacred" places of happiness.
- Such one-sided forgiveness and reconciliation is a path ... a permanent imposition ... had there not been that inner source of love that enabled this woman to live her life. Such a surplus of love is grace. A gift of a greater love, religiously speaking: the gift of a God who gives himself into this love and thus becomes a third party for us.

Initially, Mrs. Tuner did not see the fruits of her endurance bear fruit for her relationship. Other examples have taught me that one-sided reconciliation and love reached the other person only with a delay. It is

48   *The need for perspective*

precisely when we have "lived-out our love," when we have given away our love, and when it has, subjectively, fizzled out, that all of sudden something softens in the other person. In this way, many dying people live on in the bereaved:

> *One woman, for example, wore her deceased husband's scarves for many months and sometimes even his blazer. She wanted to tell him that she had now understood his love and wanted to internalize it ...*

Under which circumstances do we become scapegoated and when not? Neither those who take center stage nor those who have a strong lobby are scapegoated. If I think of my patients, some of those who were scapegoated were quiet, strong personalities. However, what can we do to avoid being hurt and crushed? The key question is: Do we manage to let others' projections stand without identifying with them? On this hinged whether or not patients cracked. Some—especially among these patients—impressed me with their power of forgiveness. Their suffering bordered on futility ... and, so I hope and believe, was not in vain after all.

2.9 What do victims need?

Perpetrators need reconciliation—but what do victims need? With victims, we do not think of reconciliation, at least not to begin with, but rather of healing, where wounds were inflicted. We think of respect where there was contempt, of appreciation, love, acceptance ... and yet none of this goes far enough. Victims need to be reached behind their many and sometimes sheer interminable injury. But how? Too much love and closeness tend to be overwhelming, just as not enough maybe, too. What is the significance of reconciliation and forgiveness?

The starting points and emotional situations of victims and perpetrators are different, although they are barely ever clearly distinguishable. I have already discussed collective one-sidedness, repression, and coming to terms with the past (Section 2.3). What follows considers these two perspectives separately: What do perpetrators need, and what do victims need? What do I need as a victim, what as a perpetrator?

Let me begin with the victim's perspective because in a society determined by self-assertiveness, many people were first victims—onto whom nameless individual and collective evil were transferred. Being a victim means being weak, speechless, and sick; it is the child's and the animal's position. Being a victim generates many defence mechanisms: withdrawal, fearing all kinds of threats. In this state, many of us feel

The need for perspective 49

isolated and not understood. The plight of the weak, of the child, and sometimes also of the animal involves being unable to tell anyone about one's distress. In particular the silence of children is often misunderstood as if they had something to hide or were partly to blame for the wrongdoing. In reality, however, children thus affected usually lack a language in which to recount the violence or deprivation they suffered. The underlying reasons are inscrutable, even for victims. Most do not understand themselves, neither in their often desperate or ambivalent reactions to their surroundings nor in their self-destruction. In their inner images, they are forlorn—as if lost in a desolate landscape.

First of all, victims need *help to understand and accept themselves*. They need to be loved and trusted in advance, for someone to stand by them (perhaps even a "fan") whatever happens, As a young teacher, I once formed a fan club for an ostracized boy in my class. It all began in private: my friends prayed for him. In class, I discussed what the suffering need and what a "fan" can achieve, of course without talking specifically about the boy concerned. One day, two girls came up to me and said that even extinct forests needed a fan club.

This first aspect also includes *impartial listening*. When he was recently awarded an honorary doctorate by the Faculty of Theology at Freiburg University, the Jesuit priest Klaus Mertes cited Jean Vanier, the Catholic theologian and philosopher, who reportedly said on his deathbed that he had "underestimated the suffering of the victims of abuse."[4] Mertes found such self-knowledge at the end of life magnificent and added: so many people talk about abuse, without understanding "that they have not understood the suffering of abuse victims, nor what the victims but also what their sufferings 'say.'" According to Mertes, our attitude towards victims is decisive: "Do not think we always understand what they are telling us." What Mertes articulates with regard to sexual abuse also holds true for anyone who, even if perhaps differently, has been severely exploited or disregarded.

Victims also need *help to endure*. They need encouragement when perseverance is required, as well as loving, embracing hands. Animals, too, can give affection. Feeling understood even when we are angry, and understanding ourselves, helps against the hardening of feelings. While anger may become a source of strength, it needs to be abated time and again. Bitterness is not worthwhile. The victim screams: "How, how, how else? How to do things otherwise?" The answer lies within us, as a secret. I often give my patients the simple word "somehow" to take with them. "You'll be amazed, it works somehow."

At some stage, victims need *generosity to forgive*. This is liberating, even if it remains an absolute imposition and must not be demanded

50 *The need for perspective*

by others. Forgiveness also means leaving open the question of fate ("why me?") and remaining susceptible to delayed answers, to delayed affirmation and love. So much quality of life ultimately hinges on such openness—and of course on such appreciation and love, indeed on being loved. This is a question to ask our world ...

Also helpful are *experiences of coping with life* and assuming responsibility, for instance, at work, in a local club, or raising a dog. A vote of confidence, "I trust you to do this," uplifts us.

How to overcome the victim's role? For some people, leaving behind old relationships and habits is important. Rahel, who was familiar with the Bible (Section 1.1.), dreamed: "You are Abraham"; for her, staying away from her parents proved to be healing. We can, of course, time and again discover our own resources and the chances that our life presents us with. Yet as many victim biographies show, doing so becomes manifoldly challenging.

Victims *need their suffering to be recognized* if they ever want to be able to leave behind their role as victims. Today, it is often supposed that this requires identifying perpetrators, as well as incriminating and punishing their actions. I am not sure whether this path is truly liberating. Not only because victims of particularly dreadful wrongdoing are condemned even more to silence and victimization. How come? Which victims? I am thinking, for example, of Satanism within one's family, of ritual violence, or abnormal practices in an entire ethnic group, all of which never surface to consciousness and of which perpetrators can never be made conscious as such. Hence, the victims of such actions, contrary to all demands, remain without jurisdiction and have not only the perpetrators but also society against them. I am, however, also skeptical about this path because I often sense a new exertion of power behind the call for jurisdiction—however important this is in individual cases. As if we were entitled to "point the finger at him or her" and to ignore the need to work on our own awareness. Jesus behaved more magnanimously and nobly in the story about the adulteress who was about to be stoned to death. Although he did not exonerate her misdemeanor, he told the people gathered around him: "Let anyone among you who is without sin be the first to throw a stone at her" (John 8:1–11).

A new future also needs *a new historiography*, which also needs to be written by the victims: this endeavor ought to begin by defining their individual biography, one that valorizes rather than debases their story. Yet we also need a historiography in the proper sense of the word, because in my view our collective still lacks adequate means for interpreting violence. We tend to think that some abuses of power

The need for perspective 51

purposefully and consciously humiliate and exploit others (e.g., as weapons of war, as means of abasement, or as "educational strategies"). In many cases, however, this is not the case. Many transgressions are *purely compensatory*, semi-conscious, or passed on from one unconscious to another, thus further degrading the victim. Abused, he or she is not even treated as a subject, but merely as a commodity—as dirt. But such an unconscious pattern, in which we work off on an innocent person what would otherwise unbearably pressure us, occurs in many more people than we might generally assume. In the dying, their dark sides ("shadows") and the vestiges of previous degradation may burst open. In both respects, the dying wish to experience themselves as integrated. Shadow integration in dying processes often occurs behind the protective backdrop of symbols: the dying clean, toss and turn, see a cleansing light, or resist being sucked into the vortex.[5] The dying need to be encouraged and reassured that they are in (and will come into) order as who they are. They wish to be allowed to be a whole person and to die as one. If it were us, would we not feel exactly the same?

It is an inner law or a psychological pattern that while sanctions protect us in the penultimate instance, they fail to do so in the final one. I say this also in view of the many crimes of incest currently being uncovered (e.g., in the Catholic Church, in schools, sports associations). Sanctions provide no "solution." They put a stop to wrongness—but ostracize new groups of people and create a new taboo. What protects and frees us in the final instance would be or is (above all) coming to consciousness—emerging from the shadow of anonymous and unconscious guilt through gaining awareness. What would develop the collective is if perpetrators—and the perpetrator aspects in each of us—would *feel* what they have done (Section 2.2).

Does shadow work also liberate the individual victim? I believe it does. I have observed that many victims become free *when* they realize that they too depend on grace—as this frees them from being hardened and entrapped in their aversion to life. Becoming aware of grace makes them deeply human and helps them to become reconciled with themselves and their own becoming. I am not thinking of the stupid question that abuse victims are asked: Was the child not "partly to blame" for being raped? What I mean instead are the consequences for adult life: when former victims later overeagerly cling to an exaggerated sense of their own innocence, when women sweepingly despise men (and vice versa), when projections and hidden aggressions are neurotically maintained and poison the body as well as the family and work atmosphere. From such attitudes may emerge new perpetrator constellations,

52 *The need for perspective*

in future generations or in a person's surroundings. Most perpetrators were once victims, yet never became free.

On the path to freedom and peace, victims also need *patience*. Repeatedly caught up by suffering, and by the sheer insurmountable consequences of the nameless, they must let themselves be helped time and again. Can they find love? Can they love themselves, and then forgive … until new circumstances and a new inner state and mode of increasingly establishing themselves? Many victims enter a new phase in their life story after a certain delay. This happens years or even decades after coming to terms with the past. Then, the will and grace to leave matters behind, and to increasingly enter the perspective of the here and now, are given all at once. What was, is now put into its context—and can remain there.

What would victims need from their perpetrators?—Insight, remorse, and a change in mindset. This rarely happens, however, especially in the case of severe guilt. That is why victims need credible models of unilateral reconciliation and forgiveness (Section 2.7). Examples include Nelson Mandela, the Holocaust survivor Eva Kor, who forgave all her tormentors including Dr. Mengele, or Aba Gayle, who made peace with her daughter's killer and is now fighting against the death penalty in Oregon (Unger, 2019). This change in mindset ultimately arises from God and no one else being the judge, which was the very meaning of the Hebrew word *shaphat* ("to pronounce sentence, God is the judge"). This word made history and gave rise to the idea that conflicts may—positively speaking—also be entrusted to God, to the consciousness of the Israelites, and thus also of our culture: may HE judge in his own time and in his own way, so that I may—as far as possible—already be free now. And may HE protect me and let wounds heal.

Amid all this, victims would actually need *God*, even if they are no longer able to believe in him. They do not need God less, but *more*: as a guarantor, as a source.

And they need *experiences of happiness*, so as to rely on the good things in this world—and to eventually be able to forgive (see the experience of hope, Section 3.3).

2.10 What do perpetrators need?

Regarding perpetrators, it is probably important that we ask this question at all. Let me be more specific and ask what they need …

- … considering their high degree of unconsciousness: What should make them want to know the truth about themselves? Do they have

The need for perspective 53

any idea about what drives them? Can they, in their affectation of power, accept that they need redemption? What would help are mature people who do not play matters down, yet nevertheless know that becoming guilty is part of life.

- … considering their incapacity to feel: what would help are people or friends who are cheerful and capable of suffering. Perpetrators need sheltered spaces in which their hidden feelings can surface, where they too can cry and where they can be shown possibilities for doing *good*. Making amends by proxy: let me do today what I can do today…
- … considering that perpetrators were usually themselves victims and whose inner child we must therefore address. A new quality of communal connectedness would be needed, as expressed by the ancient term *communio sanctorum* ("communion of saints"). Here I see both great chances for and the limitations of many, especially small churches: while sometimes managing to integrate perpetrators, they also marginalize other people.

The more perpetrators allow insight and repentance to occur (and this also applies to our own perpetrator aspects), the more they also need to experience being carried by love. They also need to be fundamentally accepted. Wrongdoing can and must be condemned, not, however, perpetrators in their innermost. They need our respect and embrace in spite of everything, as well as to be supported in approaching their victims and in asking for forgiveness.

In this respect, repentant perpetrators need to be reassured that forgiveness *exists*, even if a victim is not (yet) prepared to forgive. *One of my patients was wronged as a child by her mother. When the mother was dying, she implored her daughter to forgive her. My patient replied: "I can't forgive you yet. I'm still suffering too much from what you did … but please be assured that one day I'll be able to forgive you."* And if victims are unable or unwilling to do so, perpetrators, in order to stand up and find new self-respect, need examples of lived repentance and reversal. One such example is Claude Anshin Thomas (2004), a Vietnam War veteran now working as a Zen monk for peace and the healing of wounds caused by violence and war. Another is the convicted murderer Dieter Gurkasch, who after his release became a yoga teacher and for years wished those who had ostracized him "the very best from the bottom of his heart." In doing so, he found inner peace.[6]

Religiously speaking, we find the certainty that we will be forgiven in believing in a merciful, benevolent God (whose goodness runs deeper than any duality of good and evil). It is the faith in a God who

54   *The need for perspective*

makes renewal possible through guilt. Whenever we know we need it, redemption must be certain, a fact. One enables the other, and vice versa. Christian theology has been convincingly devised, most of all for us as perpetrators, just as its rites prove effective (Section 2.12): repentance is followed by grace, pardon, and peace. For this process of repentance to succeed, perpetrators need people around them whose reconciled existence they can feel. Nevertheless, we should not imagine cutting short pardoning processes. Repentance means feeling, which may mean waiting for years.

> *Mr Moll and his wife were ordinary people from working class families. During their childhoods, poverty and violence were part of everyday life. In Mr Moll's eyes, he had been good to his daughter, because he had promoted her athletic talent (despite a lack of money). His daughter, however, remembered her father's drinking problem and rough behaviour. He had beaten her, under the influence of alcohol but also when sober. When she was about 20 years old, (she had meanwhile moved to another country), she consulted a psychiatrist and distanced herself from her parents. She told close friends that she had been abused as a child. Her parents thought she was accusing her father of rape. In sum, daughter and parents had severed contact for 20 years.*

> *Before dying, Mr Moll wanted to come to terms with the shadow that had cast itself over his life. He accepted help from a therapist. Trusting the therapist, the daughter also came to her father's deathbed for a threeway conversation about reconciliation. In the end, she supported her father on his way towards death. His deepest wish—that his wife and daughter should stand at his grave together—came true.*

Occasionally, a deeply troubled dying person becomes aware (and can only then become aware) at their final hour of how much their partner suffered by remaining at their side. Or how bad growing up in this particular family had been for their children. If the burden of conscience breaks open and repentance occurs, this may enable all family members to experience grace, "perpetrators" and victims alike. The plea for forgiveness then comes together with the strength to forgive and with answers to a decades-long "why?"

Sometimes, repentance might happen only in death—or even later, in timelessness. We don't know. What I have experienced in my work from time to time, however, is that much later in life the victims of violence dream about their deceased perpetrators and their repentance:

The need for perspective 55

My late father sexually exploited me as a child. Then he appeared to me in a dream and looked at me deeply. I can't get rid of that look. It moves me.

Whatever the circumstances, perpetrators need the trust of others, of third parties, that they too will come to terms with their life and their guilt at some point. The many individual fates that I have encountered over the years have made me realize that perpetrators also need anonymity (a crucial aspect of Alcoholics Anonymous), that is, the opposite of self-righteous retaliation.

As I have suggested (Section 2.9), some perpetrators live through their dying process and also their guilt only symbolically. Perhaps the symbol saved them from "having to line up." Even as victims we must not forget that the truth remains incomplete—despite everything else. Perpetrators, too, need privacy and sheltered spaces. Much is allowed to remain hidden behind the scenes. The conclusion that everything must come to light for the sake of the truth may be wrong and not even necessary. Both perpetrators and victims need *God* or *the absolute* in their own way. Only *HE/IT* "knows" (see Hebrew *shaphat*, Section 2.10). "*HE*" holds the whole truth, *HE* also knows how to deal with me (confront, comfort and hold me). Ultimately, only God remains ... just as absolution only exists in the absolute (Gerl-Falkovitz, 2008, p. 195).

2.11 Forgiveness as decision: Two models from the victim's perspective

Various models have emerged from studies on reconciliation and forgiveness processes and partly also from centuries of experience. These models illumine the patterns and the process. They are very helpful in supporting those affected and contribute to a general understanding of these processes. They provide orientation and help us to walk the difficult path and to cope with any inherent spiritual challenges. Models of reconciliation teach us, for instance, not to altruistically cut short the path, and thus screen out difficult emotions. And they can make us aware of the importance of empathy, decision, or grace.

Among these diverse models, I first discuss two models that consider the victim's perspective (Worthington & Sandage, 2016; Enright, 2001). Afterwards, I discuss two models that offer perpetrators answers. I have already discussed the models developed by Stauss (2010) and von Tiedemann (2017) (Sections 1.6 and 2.6).

The model developed by Everett L. Worthington (Worthington & Sandage, 2016, pp. 7–8), an American professor of psychology, is suitable

56 *The need for perspective*

for individual, couple, and family therapy with victims. Forgiveness reduces stress and induces a shift from being unreconciled to being reconciled. Religion and spirituality are, according to Worthington, part of every relationship (e.g., between victim and perpetrator, between the victim and the sacred). A positive therapeutic relationship helps to make forgiveness possible. Worthington (Worthington & Sandage, 2016, p. 16) distinguishes five phases:

> **R = Recall the hurt.** To heal, you have to face the fact that you've been hurt. Make up your mind not to be spiteful, not to treat yourself like a victim, and not to treat the other person like a jerk. Decide to forgive. Decide that you are not seeking payback, but will treat others as valuable.

> **E = Empathize with your partner.** Empathy means putting yourself in the other person's chair. Pretend they are sitting in an empty chair across from you. Talk to them. Pour your heart out. Then, when you've had your say, sit in their chair. Talk back to the imaginary you in a way that helps you see why the other person might have wronged you. This builds empathy, and even if you can't empathize, you might feel more sympathy, compassion, or love, which helps you heal from hurt. This allows you to give ... I would add that empathy and emotional reprocessing are also important for leaving behind the traumatic perspective.[7]

> **A = Altruistic gift.** Give forgiveness as an unselfish, altruistic gift. All of us remember when we wronged someone—for instance, a parent, a teacher, or a friend—and that person forgave us. We felt light and free. And we didn't want to disappoint them by doing wrong again. By forgiving unselfishly, you can give that same gift to someone who hurt you.

> **C = Commit.** Once you've forgiven, write a note to yourself—something as simple as, "Today, I forgave [person's name] for hurting me." This helps your forgiveness last.

> **H = Hold onto forgiveness.** We write notes of commitment because we will almost surely be tempted to doubt that we really forgave. We can re-read our notes. We did forgive.[8]

What impresses me about Worthington's model is how strongly determined people seem to be to forgive, give, and remember their forgiveness. Equally impressive is that Worthington acknowledges that altruism is necessary. The strength of his model is perhaps also its

The need for perspective 57

weakness: How do victims become willing to forgive? And what if the hurt is simply tremendous? What if they are aware, yet only diffusely? Spirituality also remains vague (at least to me) in Worthington's model and its potential is unrecognized.

Robert D. Enright (2001), the founder of international forgiveness research, has also developed a much-cited model. Conceived as a coping strategy, his model, aimed at victims, wants to help them find their way out of the prison of negative emotions (grief, anger, fear, despair, hatred of perpetrators and themselves). For Enright, forgiveness offers the chance to overcome blockage and to regain trust in oneself and others. He distinguishes four phases and encourages self-reflection (see Enright, 2001, p. 78, "guideposts for forgiving").

1 Uncovering your anger (and also injury; my addition) (uncovering phase).

- How have you avoided dealing with anger?
- Have you faced your anger?
- Are you afraid to expose your shame and guilt?
- Has your anger affected your health?
- Have you been obsessed with the injury or the offender?
- Do you compare your situation with the offender's?
- Has the injury caused a permanent change in your life?
- Has the injury changed your worldview?

2 Deciding to forgive (decision phase).

- Decide that what you have been doing hasn't worked.
- Be willing to begin the forgiveness process.
- Decide to forgive.

3 Working on forgiveness (work phase).
The negative feelings towards the offender can gradually be replaced by positive ones (compassion, generosity, possibly love). Essentially, this happens through empathy (see Enright & Fitzgibbons, 2015, pp. 74–76).

- Work towards understanding.
- Work towards compassion.
- Accept the pain.
- Give the offender a gift.

58 *The need for perspective*

4   Discovery and release from the emotional prison (deepening phase)

- Discover the meaning of your suffering.
- Discover your need for forgiveness.
- Discover that you are not alone.
- Discover the purpose of your life.
- Discover the freedom of forgiveness

What impresses me about Enright's model is how he circumscribes anger, as well as encourages decision-making and the humility to work on forgiving. Similar to Worthington's model, I have reservations about the depth of Enright's approach: Where is the reference to grace? How does what people cannot "do" happen, that is, transformation in the depths of our soul? Where it would in fact be necessary.

2.12 Deliverance from guilt: Two models from the perpetrator's perspective

2.12.1 First model: Twelve-step program of alcoholics anonymous

The *Twelve Steps Program of Alcoholics Anonymous (AA)* is different from the models discussed in the previous section. The AA model was founded around 1935 by two Americans who themselves had a drinking problem. In 1939, one of the founders, William Griffith Wilson, wrote down the experiences of the then young community as a 12-step program. Perhaps because it emerged at an earlier time, or perhaps because it is aimed at *perpetrators* who are aware of their guilt, the AA program refers to the grace of a higher power, and explicitly stresses that human beings are dependent on this higher power. This approach offers the chance for profound change. The 12 steps are as follows:[9]

1   We admit that we are powerless over our own problem. This may be substance dependence or, depending on the group's topic, other problems. We admit that we can no longer cope with our "daily life."
2   Come to believe that only a Power greater than ourselves can restore us to sanity. Originally the word "God" was introduced here for the "Power greater than oneself." In order to open up groups also to non-religious persons, the new wording was chosen.
3   Decide to entrust our will and life to the care of God as each of us understands Him.

The need for perspective   59

4 Make a searching and fearless inventory of ourselves.
5 Admit to ourselves and to someone else the exact nature of our wrongs.
6 Be ready to have God remove all behavior that obstructs life.
7 Humbly ask God to remove "all personal behavior chronically obstructing life."
8 Make a list of all persons we have harmed and become willing to make amends to them.
9 Make direct amends to such people wherever possible, except when doing so would injure them or others.
10 Continue to make the "inner inventory" and admit when you are wrong.
11 Seek through "prayer and meditation" to improve our deep and conscious contact with God, as we understand Him, and pray for knowledge, to see His will and the power to carry that out.
12 After this "spiritual awakening" (i.e., how we have used these steps for ourselves and live by them), pass on the message to others affected, and stay guided in our daily life by the principles of the respective twelve-step group.

2.12.2 Second model: Liturgy of the Eucharist

Unlike the AA program, the second "model" does not explicitly provide help for perpetrators, but still proves extremely effective, especially for people with real guilt: *the Eucharist*, the rite of the Catholic Church. The Eucharistic Prayer or Mass—at least in the Western Church—offers us answers "from the perpetrator's perspective." Behind both the ecclesiastical rite and the sacrament of confession lies an astonishingly consistent thought process about "deliverance from guilt," including forgiveness. If for once we do not object to the missing perspective of the victim, then these sacraments or rites are almost exemplary and consistent with the process of reconciliation.

The Liturgy of the Eucharist,[10] still celebrated in the Catholic Church to this day, proceeds in several distinct phases: opening, liturgy of the Word, Eucharistic celebration, and dismissal. The process unfolds via the admission of guilt, and thereby losing the relationship with God, to healing this relationship or human connectedness, in which Jesus is seen as a mediator. Mostly, the rite is based on the unspoken equation according to which Jesus gave himself to make amends for our guilt (Anselm of Canterbury's Theory of Satisfaction). Quite apart from the fact that this equation—abbreviated thus—is incompatible with Jesus's extraordinary behavior (Renz, 2020), the rite

60 *The need for perspective*

initially leaves many believers unmoved. Why? We—or rather most of us—were victims before we became guilty; we enter the place of worship with a yearning that corresponds to our victim status. Yet the rite is an answer to guilt. It is shaped by a collective history of guilt and by corresponding historiography (of the Israelites, who interpreted the destruction of the temple and the dispersion of the people not as a tragedy but as guilt). Here, however, I wish to help readers understand the rite as an ingenious answer to guilt and the perpetrator's position:

1   In the opening, those who are prepared become conscious of their own guilt and need for redemption, as well as conscious of the sacredness of God, who is able to turn everything around. The opening begins with coming inwardly before God and fostering the unity of the congregation: the sign of the cross reminds the congregation of the Lord's presence. The Kyrie invokes Jesus as Kyrios (i.e., Jesus Christ is our Lord and God). Those who now approach God become aware of their wrongdoings and shortcomings: these are brought before God by the individual in an admission of guilt, as well as by the congregation as a whole, followed by the promise of reconciliation granted by God. The Gloria is devoted to reflecting on God's glory (Gloria is the Latin translation of Hebrew *kabod*, "abundance, honor, glory," and of Greek *doxa*, "he alone deserves the honor." It is followed by silence and prayer.

   Comment: I am impressed by how much this rite is based on reverence (the sacredness of God) and by how self-evidently human beings are allowed to be human. Everything is designed to touch and heal them. This is a very beautiful thought, assuming that our perpetrator aspects here become apparent.

2   In the liturgy of the word, we come to the scriptures chosen for this day and their interpretation. The texts, selected mostly from the Old and New Testaments, are related to each other.

   Comment: The interpretation of scripture addresses us as reasoning persons: Can we understand what we believe? Whenever this happens, the subsequent profession of faith amounts to us saying "yes." We thus open ourselves up. In the intercessions, we long for peace, healing, redemption—each in our own way and as a worldwide congregation.

3   In the Eucharistic celebration, what we long for *takes place*: the transformation of the human soul.[11] In the preparation of gifts, our own life is brought before God in the form of bread and wine, in the knowledge that what happens outside is an image of what should happen inside. Wine, mixed with water, represents the

The need for perspective 61

interwovenness of the divine and the human. The Eucharistic Prayer leads to Jesus's words at the Lord's Supper. They are the words of transformation, which are followed by the praise of the congregation, by the Lord's Prayer, by the greeting of peace and by the Agnus Dei ("Lamb of God, you take away the sin of the world, have mercy on us"). Communion, representing Jesus's devotion, can be received at all times and in all places.

Comment: The subject here is grace and transformation, which involves more than coaching or following a path. If I assume that people have previously truly attained their longing for salvation, then this is where God sacramentally becomes one with us. What is accepted, is forgiven (on the metaphor of the Lamb of God, see Renz, 2020; Schenker, 2001).

4　Dismissal as affirmation and blessing. This also concerns living the peace received.

Comment: In this rite, the Church, unlike the state, also performs an emotional task: it *reminds* us of Jesus and *celebrates* his legacy. The rite means *more* than the inclusion of music and gestures, and more than a self-forged ritual. It arose from ancient needs, longings, and healing experiences with Jesus. The rite therefore speaks the language of our preconscious and unconscious and has the potential to reach our longings, which lie waiting there. This also applies to the theme of reconciliation, forgiveness, and the need for peace and solidarity (Section 1.6; Stauss, 2010); indeed precisely to this—because it is our original connectedness that we have lost at some point.

We need the rite, but also an interpretation based on it that "spells out" the redeeming nature of Jesus, and that no longer focuses one-sidedly on the cross, nor one-sidedly addresses perpetrators (the perpetrator inside me), but which gauges redemption in terms of Jesus's absolutely sovereign and groundbreaking behavior.

As victims, we would need words such as tragedy, apology, appreciation, and meaning. From the victim's perspective, the divine service would also be about rediscovering the reconnection to God, about sustenance, strengthening, and experiencing God. And yet, the path towards such reconnection would need to lead through being touched, through words such as freedom, recognition, and gratitude. A God who honors (!) victims in their suffering, reconstitutes their dignity, and perhaps even asks us to let go of our wounds rather than encapsulate and armor ourselves (i.e., the original meaning of sin). A God who asks us to open ourselves again completely.

62 *The need for perspective*

But are such a God and such a divine service conceivable? Let me turn the question around: Are they inconceivable? Does this not correspond to Jesus's intention and behavior and to God's avowal of him—precisely in his suffering? A God who so deeply absorbs, accepts, and transforms our wounds?

Notes

1 Müller-Fahrenholz (1996, pp. 21–22) speaks of an embezzlement of the Christian message, which (among other aspects) is exclusively perpetrator focused.
2 Individuation is a concept devised by C.G. Jung (*Collected Works*, 1957–1992) and means isolation or becoming oneself. Not, however, in the sense of autonomy and so-called self-determination, which are often misunderstood today, but rather in terms of inner maturation. Jung had in mind the mature human being as an inner objective.
3 The subcategories that referred to "the third" (based on experiences of hope) were as follows:

- Finally, someone who understands and appreciates. Experiencing love through a third party/us;
- Finding words, managing to articulate injuries;
- Structural changes, a new boss, mediator;
- Satisfaction. An important conversation with the other side took place;
- "I'm doing it for the sake of others/the children."

The subcategories based on decisions were as follows:

- Clearing the air, "now or never." An act of will, prepared to engage in a process, accepts therapeutic and spiritual help;
- Talking to the conflict party, in the presence of a neutral auxiliary;
- Praying for the other person or for one's own openness;
- Engaging in dialogue with God, haggling: for the sake of a third party

4 Vanier was devastated when his mentor, Father Philippe, was accused of sexually abusing young women. When a television documentary in early March 2019 allowed witnesses to speak for the first time, Vanier was already too weak to express his views. But he had already formulated this admission before.
5 This does not, however, mean that a dark side is lurking whenever a dying person sees such images and acts out their disquiet. I question any hasty interpretations in this respect.
6 Bleisch and Bossart (moderators) (2018, May 21). Sternstunde der Nacht: In the wake of evil [Video Podcast]. Retrieved from https://www.srf.ch/kultur/gesellschaft-religion/wochenende-gesellschaft/sternstunde-der-nacht-das-boese-zwischen-abscheu-und-anziehung.

The need for perspective   63

7 Empathy and emotional reprocessing are also important in trauma treatment. They are central to the EMDR (Eye Movement Disensitization and Reprocessing) approach.

8 Retrieved from http://www.evworthington-forgiveness.com/reach-forgiveness-of-others.

9 See www.alcohol.org/alcoholics-anonymous (with minor stylistic adjustments).

10 Retrieved with omissions and adjustments from Information by the Communications Department of the United States Conference of Catholic Bishops https://ourcatholicfaith.org/mass/eucharist.html and from the Archdiocese of Vienna.

11 In this context, I leave aside the subject of transubstantiation (transformation of bread and wine into the body and blood of Christ). For my interpretation of Jesus as Christ, see Renz, 2017 and 2020.

3 The five-phase reconciliation process

Reconciliation and forgiveness are complex processes. What leads to the turning point? Several good models of reconciliation and forgiveness have been developed over the years. So what made me look for yet another model? I was interested in the processes of forgiveness and reconciliation that occur deep inside patients, particularly as they approach death. How should we imagine, and how might we understand these processes and their unfolding? Do they consist of particular, recurring stages? I raised these questions also with my depth psychological way of thinking in mind.

Many observations at deathbeds, of an inner urging, have alerted me to the existence of patterns, for instance, the meaning of crises, but also of turning points. The word catastrophe, from Greek, means "sudden turn, turning around, overturning." But is that all? Did the processes in the observed patients reach a turning point merely due to crises? What exactly changed? What emerged? What was so different afterwards than before?

The phase model presented in this book may help people in their victimhood (i.e., woundedness) and in their perpetratorhood.[1] They want to be redeemed from both conditions. Over time, I have learned to distinguish five phases:

1 Denial or avoidance
2 Crisis
3 Experiences of hope
4 Decision
5 Reconciliation and forgiveness

3.1 Denial or avoidance

Reconciliation processes begin when we are unreconciled. This itself is a proposition. Development begins amid denial or avoidance when we are embroiled and entangled with ourselves. The German language

DOI: 10.4324/9781003310907-4

The five-phase reconciliation process   65

contrasts two closely related terms in this respect: *Verwicklung* (embroilment, being caught up with a dense emotional underbrush) and *Entwicklung* (development). Denial and avoidance are frequent patterns of behavior, in daily life (anyway) and even in severe illness. In our study, only 10 out of 50 patients with a major conflict showed no denial and avoidance. Our study only referred to denial as described by Elisabeth Kübler-Ross. In 30 cases, the reconciliation and forgiveness process began with this stage. Of a total of 660 protocol entries, 107 were assigned to denial. Looking at society as a whole suggests that many people tend to brush aside their conflicts all their lives—either by denying or by avoiding them.

At the same time, we are often only partly aware of such denied conflicts. In everyday language, we also speak of repression (in our study, this was true of 76 of the 107 observations mentioned above). Some patients behaved unnaturally cheerfully; others lived as if preprogrammed, became cynical, expressed a sense of futility or suicidal desire, or vented their anger at others. Projections arose. As caregivers, physicians, and therapists, we realized that something was troubling these patients, despite their total unawareness. If these patients confirmed our impression, even nonverbally (e.g., by nodding), we also recorded these assessments (the above-mentioned 76 cases).

Thus, we are affected by serious conflicts (with others, with ourselves, with fate) long before we consciously address them. We suffer when things smolder. Some of us, masters of the art of repression, seem to make our way through life quite well with this strategy. The repressed "is placed on hold" and no longer troubles the affected person. However, someone close to them (e.g., their wife, husband, or mother) may often suffer even more, finding themselves embroiled in projections. We often scapegoat those close to us when we repress conflicts and anger. And yet, in severe illness, our coping strategies might change. Many dying people are no longer able to repress as well as they used to.

Conflict often affects our energy. This already happens when we are in semi-conscious denial. Some people feel extremely tired or are stewing. Whom or what is their anger directed at? Who or what is vexing them or sapping their energies? If we are doing our utmost to repress, we will not really want to know. We do not want to be disturbed. We might become bitter or hard—and yet, in this state, we are never free. Elisabeth Kübler-Ross, the pioneer of near-death studies, explored maturing processes in dying and aptly described the first phase as denial (1969).

66 *The five-phase reconciliation process*

Conscious denial, which mostly amounts to avoidance, is less frequent. It occurs when we dismiss a conflict because tackling it seems pointless, at least at that moment (31 out of 107). We avoid conflicts for different reasons: there is no one who might intervene and mediate; we are so hurt that we would only overreact; illness has sapped our energy, and we are simply not strong enough. Besides, the person we are grappling with does not seem to see reason. Conscious avoidance, and our conscious attempt to repress, serve to maintain quality of life in the here and now. They are often key life strategies, for months and years, and essential for survival.

Our study distinguished various subcategories, which could be ticked on the observation chart given in Table 3.1.

Denial or avoidance sometimes seamlessly blends into reconciliation, and vice versa. In our study, 4 patients died during or after denial. This, too, can be a good way to die.

> *Mr Bocca, a second-generation Italian, was hospitalized because he was suffering from pain and an infection. During anamnesis, he told me that repression helped him. Religion meant nothing to him, except in the broadest sense. Nor had God helped. Mr Bocca mentioned, rather impromptu, that he had been out of touch with his sister in Italy for years, which troubled him. Their severed contact went back to a conflict with his brother-in-law. Still, Mr Bocca consciously kept avoiding the conflict: one couldn't reason with the other side anyway, he said (conscious denial).*

Table 3.1 Denial (Kübler-Ross: denial)

Coping	Semi-conscious: repression, wanting peace, playing things down	☐
	Conscious: "I will wait with reconciliation"; not the right time, no mediator	☐
Emotional	Semi-conscious: cynical, offended, hardened, "turned off"	☐
	Conscious: hurt/injury has been retriggered, fearing it	☐
Physical	Semi-conscious: tired, lacking drive, blocked	☐
	Conscious: "I feel too ill/weak for reconciliation"	☐
Relationships	Semi-conscious: breaking off contact, exerting power, self-victimization	☐
	Conscious: "I am consciously avoiding others," "I am not ready yet"; the other side ("opponent, adversary") cannot see reason	☐
Spiritual	Semi-conscious: futility, emptiness	☐
	Conscious: waiting for grace; "... God has to help"	☐

The five-phase reconciliation process   67

Eleven days later: Mr Bocca had meanwhile grown completely disinterested in his surroundings and wanted to be left alone. He was tired and apathetic (unconscious denial). Two days later, he repeated (unsolicited) his wish to be left alone. Yet another two days later, still nothing had changed. He remained tired and apathetic.

Four days later, the day he was discharged, Mr Bocca seemed peaceful and comfortable. Had he achieved reconciliation, or was he still repressing? (In such cases, we avoid asking questions and leave the nursing staff to record unconscious reconciliation on the observation chart).

Six weeks later: after moving quickly and unexpectedly towards death, Mr Bocca came for an outpatient consultation: I asked him whether he wished to address and resolve anything in particular. He said, quite peacefully, that there had never been a conflict with his sister, nor with his brother-in-law, nor with his family. He seemed to have totally repressed or resolved the problem within himself. The attending nurse again recorded unconscious reconciliation on the observation chart.

A week later, Mr Bocca was admitted to hospital with respiratory distress. He was restless and given highly dosed medication. Given his physical symptoms, I cautiously addressed the difficulties with his sister and brother-in-law. He dismissed me gruffly and wanted to be left in peace. The nurse recorded unconscious denial on the observation chart. Mr Bocca died the same night.

3.2 Crisis

No process without crisis—even if reconciliation and forgiveness are concerned. In our study, only 2 patients did *not* undergo crisis. A considerable number of observations, 159 out of 660, indicated a state of crisis or aggravation. As a rule, crises occur repeatedly (37 out of 50 patients in our study; see Figures 1 and 2, Appendix). Every change in patients' physical condition or family circumstances may precipitate a crisis. Conflicts, moreover, accumulate. Patients often feel unreconciled—with someone else, with themselves, with their illness, as well as with God, with fate, or with the "Eternal Thou" (see Stauss; see also Section 1.6), all at the same time. In our study, 20 reconciliation processes began directly in the midst of crisis (perhaps due to hospitalization).

Staying in hospital is per se a crisis, at least physically. Patients feel deprived of their everyday routine (and ability to do things) and maybe suffering severe pain. Their future is uncertain. All patients in our study

68 The five-phase reconciliation process

assumed that they might die soon, even those who lived at least longer than expected.[2] The more certain the prospect of death, the more urgent reconciliation processes become. Whenever patients managed to live well again, at least for a while (see Mrs Casutt, Section 3.4; Figure 2, Appendix), or whenever denial or pseudo-reconciliation once more gained the upperhand, then crises, reconciliation, and forgiveness urged patients again in their final days and hours. This also happened in Mr. Ladner's case (see Figure 1, Appendix):[3]

> *Mr Ladner was hospitalized and then transferred to outpatient care and therapy. He told me how wearying he found the never-ending conflict with his wife. She, too, was suffering from cancer. He had looked after her as long as he could, but she had accepted no other help. Illness also made matters worse, "... what a life." Repression, on the one hand, and deep relationships, on the other, had helped Mr Ladner come to terms with his illness. Religion and spirituality were "nonsense," he told me.[4] He went through all the stages of the reconciliation process, from repression to a willingness to engage ... until the first family therapy session involving him, his wife and his daughter took place (see the first occurrence of 5d). I served as a bridge for the Ladners to cross saying: "Mrs Ladner, it's very kind of you to come. Your husband loves you very much and is worried about you." Expressing Mr Ladner's concern on his behalf, I asked his wife: "Who will look after you when he dies?" She started crying, sat down next to her husband, and let herself be caressed. She said in a low voice that her sister would be there for her. She accepted my offer to seek professional help. This moved and relieved Mr Ladner so much that he immediately became somnolent and began breathing intermittently. For over half an hour, we thought he was going to die. Peace. A nurse came, handed over to another nurse, and Mr Ladner fell into a crisis, inwardly and outwardly. He gesticulated and projected: "Why couldn't I die?" You (i.e., we specialists) should have done better! Three days later, I addressed the crisis: with his wife, among us professionals, with him, and now also with God. The difficult emotions became more conscious. Mr Ladner felt as if he had been rejected by God. But God was far away.*

> *Mr Ladner oscillated several times between crisis and reconciliation. —On one occasion, husband, wife, and daughter were reunited. The mood was tense. None of us quite knew what they were arguing about ... When the senior physician came, Mr Ladner vented his anger, blaming the doctor that people were unable to die there! After all, he (the doctor) was in charge ... Mr Ladner grew tired ... and the family agreed:*

The five-phase reconciliation process 69

this ward was a bad place to die. The Ladners tenderly held hands. Reconciliation? (5a). Probably not. Two hours later, Mr Ladner grew restless. He nodded when I uttered the word "crisis"—as if he wished to make one last attempt, yet first needed to experience hope. He was touched by how loving and appreciative the nurses and doctors were "despite everything." Just how conscious he was of his outburst was an open question. Be that as it was. —An hour later, as if an electric bolt had shot through his body, Mr Ladner took one last decision: he wanted to say "yes"—to himself, to how things had gone, and also to God. Saying yes, he now moved through his symptoms, became peaceful (5c), somnolent, and died, a mere three hours later.

Reconciliation and forgiveness processes intensify increasingly toward death. This is characteristic, and yet should not be confounded with what I have described elsewhere as specific to death: a change in consciousness (see Renz, 2015). As a rule, reconciliation processes press forward and occur in the here and now, before the change in consciousness that is caused by death. Sometimes, reconciliation and forgiveness seem to happen "instead of" a change in consciousness. But why "instead of"? How should we understand this? Might we understand the fact that the dying "actively" wait for reconciliation, which sometimes includes their struggle near death? Ought we then understand this struggle as a "final coming to an inner truth and consciousness"? As what—finally— enhances their dignity? Crisis, in this sense, means "waiting." At times, it seems as if merely the body were waiting.

In our study, out of those 45 patients who passed away after achieving reconciliation 22 died *within 48 hours*. Another 6 became somnolent immediately after reconciliation. This finding is consistent with my earlier observation that family processes (and thus reconciliation) are very important initially, yet suddenly become surprisingly unimportant as consciousness changes (see Renz, 2015). Interestingly, in our first study, persons who were worried or needed reconciliation were an exception. They seemed to wait, to want to wait, and to resist somnolence because peace mattered so much to them (see Renz et al., 2013).

In contrast to the first phase of denial or avoidance, in our study crises and escalations were as a rule experienced consciously (87 out of 159 protocol entries). What chances do such crises present? They accelerate maturation processes and bring conflicts to light, out of waiting, out of repression. A crisis reveals what was smoldering. The powerlessness of being sick, a lonely night, or a weekend in the hospital without visitors surface the unconscious in their own way.

70 The five-phase reconciliation process

Mr Kocic was barely responsive, yet didn't die. Whenever his daughter entered his room, he grew restless. She asked me that if her father was no more than a husk, why couldn't this body die? "Perhaps he's more than a body," I replied. Ignoring his restlessness, I asked about her father's life, his joys and worries. When she mentioned his illegitimate son, Mr Kocic grew even more restless. His daughter also noticed this and was prepared to contact her half-brother.

Mrs Nöcker had been out of touch with her brother for years. In the palliative care unit, growing weaker and weaker, she wrote her brother a letter about herself, her illness, and how their losing sight of each other pained her. Her brother didn't reply, which threw Mrs Nöcker into crisis. Her therapist tried to establish contact, but in vain. But then, Mrs Nöcker received a surprising visit from her brother. She died three days later.

Mrs Hatt, a down-to-earth woman with two young adult daughters, had suffered from anxiety disorders since being diagnosed with metastatic bowel cancer. Initially, she was afraid of dying, of the symptoms before dying. In a family meeting, in which I told Mrs Hatt about my research experience and knowledge of "dying as a transition" (Renz, 2015), she managed to find peace. The fact that good cancer treatment was a realistic proposition also helped.

A year later, Mrs Hatt told me that she had gone on living quite well (repression had worked). Now, though, the cancer was progressing quickly. Chemotherapy had served its purpose, and her fears had returned. She described her most recent anxiety attack: while she was driving, her head began feeling as if a thousand ants were crawling inside, leaving her dizzy and flustered. Why? Fearing for their mother, her daughters had been unable to work for months. Mrs Hatt continued to describe her feelings ... until I asked her whether she had experienced abuse or violence in the past. Not really, she didn't really know, although she had been asked this before. I played some music and guided Mrs Hatt into active imagination, starting from how her head had felt when was she driving. Did she see any colours? "Yes, a black-and-white pattern." Did she smell anything? Yes, olive oil, but she hadn't been able to eat any for a long time. Could she see the oil? Was it in the salad dressing? No, someone was rubbing their knees with it. The ant feeling grew stronger. Dizziness! Intestinal noises. "What do you see now?" I asked directly. No answer. "Is it a man or a woman?" "A woman! I'm about four years old, not yet in kindergarten."

The five-phase reconciliation process 71

She became dizzy and almost fell off her chair. I gave her breathing instructions. I appreciated her great effort in becoming aware, yet nevertheless pursued the issue, detail after detail. All of a sudden, Mrs Hatt exclaimed: "... the aunt who went in and out of my mother's home. She was alone with me ... Everything has turned white." I invited Mrs Hatt to look closely at this whiteness, whether it soothed or neutralized her. I made her repeat her statements and then slowly guided her back to the present. Mrs Hatt endured her vision and believed it. For weeks the focus shifted to believing her body. Meanwhile one daughter had found work again. Months later, again triggered by the crisis caused by her illness, Mrs Hatt wanted to make peace with the past, except for her aunt, who had died in the meantime. Another few months later, when she was about to die, another crisis overwhelmed her: fear, restlessness, fear. After music-assisted active imagination, which had brought her close to God (resplendent white!), she decided: "I want inner peace, also with my deceased aunt." Mrs Hatt began practising forgiveness, uttering the words "Yes, yes, yes" to her breathing rhythm. The next day, she grew calm and somnolent, and died a few days later in the presence of her daughters.

Crises manifest on different levels in reconciliation processes: beha-viorally (coping), emotionally, physically, in relationships, and spiri-tually. Accordingly, our study included various subcategories (Table 3.2).

Table 3.2 **Crisis** (Kübler-Ross: anger)

Coping	Semi-conscious: repression, wanting peace, playing things down	☐
	Conscious: "I will wait with reconciliation"; not the right time, no mediator	☐
Emotional	Semi-conscious: cynical, offended, hardened, "turned off"	☐
	Conscious: hurt/injury has been retriggered, fearing it	☐
Physical	Semi-conscious: tired, lacking drive, blocked	☐
	Conscious: "I feel too ill/weak for reconciliation"	☐
Relationships	Semi-conscious: breaking off contact, exerting power, self-victimization	☐
	Conscious: "I am consciously avoiding others," "I am not ready yet"; the other side ("opponent, adversary") cannot see reason	☐
Spiritual	Semi-conscious: futility, emptiness	☐
	Conscious: waiting for grace; "... God has to help"	☐

72 *The five-phase reconciliation process*

3.3 Experiences of hope (or the factor of grace)

Reconciliation processes are not only driven by the level of suffering, nor are they merely oriented towards our own suffering. This is one of the core messages of this book. For reconciliation, and especially for forgiveness, to occur, there needs to be some sort of extrinsic motivation. Using the example of Jesus, the promise that "the kingdom of God has come near" preceded the call to repentance and contemplation (Mark 1:15). One is closely related to the other as if the heavenly kingdom enables repentance. In our study, almost all patients (46 out of 50) had one or more experiences of hope (see Table 1: Characteristics of Sample, Appendix; Figures 1 and 2).[5] What did these experiences involve?

A patient who flatly refused to approach her son (he had hurt her too much) dreamed of a thousand white roses. They fell from the heavens while she saw herself and her son. This feeling, of falling roses, was so beautiful, and associated with such lightness, that this woman was able to tackle the conflict and write her son a card.

A man locked in an insoluble conflict with his wife had the prospect of a large gift (and thus of perspective): he would inherit 200,000 Swiss francs. He had some ideas about what to do with the money: to get a mortgage and buy a house, which he would love to manage ... and suddenly he felt he could approach his wife. He wanted to tell her this and make peace. She, too, should be able to enjoy having the house.

A seriously ill, pain-ridden, distinguished woman was so unwell that she did not want to make peace with herself or with God. She dreamed of making a child from India happy. She remembered her trip to India and the many poor children she had met there whose happiness had impressed her so deeply. She knew instantly whom she would leave her money to and approached an organization that supported Indian orphanages. She had found a vision ... a perspective beyond herself. She had also found inner peace. Even hours later, the pain had subsided for several days, much longer than usual.

The observation chart that we used in our study included many subcategories of experiencing hope is shown in Table 3.3. These categories describe what had induced hope or what it conveyed. The nurses often took handwritten notes about what that hope contained, as the above examples have shown.

The five-phase reconciliation process 73

Table 3.3 Experience of hope, motivation, something encourages reconciliation

Coping	Finding words, being able to formulate one's injury/guilt	□
	At long last, someone understands and appreciates one; feeling loved by someone/ourselves	□
Emotional	Re-establishing contact with one's feelings, "things begin to flow"	□
	"I am doing it for the sake of others/my children"; devotion	□
	Others' suffering relativizes one's own suffering	□
Physical	Pain and symptom relief, good medication (i.e., "I am able to continue)	□
Relationships	Structural changes: family structure, a new boss, a mediator	□
	"Satisfaction"/fulfillment: important discussion with the other side	□
	Being surprised by the other side/adversary: discussion, gift, gesture	□
Spiritual	Dream, spiritual experience	□
	Music-assisted relaxation, relaxation, prayer, religious ritual	□
	Longing for/willing to make peace occurs near death	□
	Experience: I am forgiven; God is merciful	□
	Synchronicity: Case review, others' prayers, "something" happened	□

The experience of hope took great effect. It enabled patients to take an initial decision to seek reconciliation (in 19 cases), but also led directly to initial reconciliation (in 24 cases). Even immediately before dying, the experience of hope often transitioned directly into initial reconciliation (also in 24 cases).

How should we interpret these results, and what ought we conclude from them? In many cases, I was impressed how quickly reconciliation and forgiveness suddenly became possible provided something really new, internal or real, presented itself as an option.

At the same time, we need to understand these figures in the context of approaching death: for it is precisely then and thereupon that reconciliation and forgiveness occur—as if a person's best qualities resurface at that point. And as if death itself epitomizes new hope. But does it really? If it does, then we cannot see this with our eyes. And yet, from the perspective of the dying, I would ask: doesn't it? In other words: hoping for peace, for a categorically different mode of being?

We need hope—whether in the midst of a life or before death. It is unusual to demand hope in reconciliation therapy, as well as in end-of-life care or palliative care. And yet, it is one of our most important findings. Consequently, the work of reconciliation means strengthening

74 *The five-phase reconciliation process*

people's hope: How, then, might we enable experiences of hope, convey hope and awaken a person's slumbering hopes? How does death become the gateway to new hope?

3.4 Decision

It is a decision to forgive and reconcile. We either want to or we don't. This is true at least in the middle of life. Accordingly, decision features prominently in models of coping and in therapy (e.g., Enright, 2001; Worthington & Sandage, 2016; see Section 2.11). The entire process belongs to what I call decision.

Thus, in our study, we were even more surprised to observe decision in "only" 31 out of 50 patients. Did the decision occur unnoticed in the other 19 patients—or not at all? Did these patients, rather than communicating a decision, just live it? The answer proves elusive. As death approaches, events come thick and fast. In our study, 16 patients, all of whom had made a decision once or several times during the process, seemed to skip this step as they moved towards death. Had they already internalized it?

Although rare, decision is—qualitatively—the alpha and omega of forgiveness and reconciliation. In our study, some patients decided to forgive and seek reconciliation once and for all. Decisions increased the awareness with which patients approached the process—and accordingly the quality of reconciliation, forgiveness, and reunion. Decision satisfied or cheered patients already during the process. They felt relieved or even fulfilled once they had taken this hurdle—to say "yes"—without escaping through the back door. Later, 15 patients emphasized that saying "yes" had helped; two made this point twice—reminding me of how the well-known theologian Karl Rahner describes this fundamental decision.[6]

> *As a dying politician put it: he had prepared his last speech, which he could no longer give himself, and was surprised that he was "utterly determined to love." He said this meant the same as "a big yes."*
>
> *One woman equated this "yes" with "finding one's way into prayer." Saying yes filled her prayers, and those filled her nights.*
>
> *Mrs Casutt's reconciliation process was impressive (see Figure 2, Appendix). I had been seeing Mrs Casutt as an out-patient for some time: she was a harsh woman with a keen eye. Deep relationships as well as God were important for her. Years ago, after an accident, she had a near-death experience with an experience of*

The five-phase reconciliation process 75

God: she saw a unique light and felt the warmth of being borne. Now, this feeling sometimes returned. She was suffering from metastatic cancer of the bladder. At the beginning of our study, Mrs Casutt was in denial (see Figure 2, Appendix). Her body and voice had hardened: her doctor had advised her to tackle whatever mattered to her. She told me that she was embroiled in several conflicts: with her husband, with her mother, and with her illness, but she didn't want to address matters. She argued that they were neither willing to discuss matters nor ready for reconciliation. She added: "Leave God out of this."

A few weeks later, the conflicts came to a head. Crisis. She told me that her husband found her illness difficult to bear. And that he reproachfully told her "that he had married a young woman so that he could die before" her. The situation with her mother wasn't any better: she wanted her to go to church more often. Mrs Casutt felt under pressure, emotionally abused and guilty—yet unnecessarily. Besides, God was far away. The following week, she began putting her difficulties into perspective: what was her husband's share, what her mother's, what her own? She had changed, touched by the face of a young patient whom she just had seen walking around the palliative care unit: "She's a lovely person, why should she have to die?" Active imagination, starting from the young woman's eyes, allowed Mrs Casutt to relax deeply. Once again, she saw "her" light (near-death experience) and found hope. Although she had no answers, she believed that suffering made sense after all. Our conversations made her feel appreciated. Strangely, during active imagination, the light praised her.

Finally, a month later, Mrs Casutt decided to talk to her husband in my presence. The decision made her happy. Two weeks later, the Casutts entered the therapy room five or six feet apart. I thanked Mr Casutt for coming and made a point of asking him about his current situation. I added that it was normal for events to come thick and fast as his wife's cancer progressed. I suggested that they both do an empathy exercise. It took effect: Mrs Casutt managed to feel her husband's latent despair. During the exercise, she was surprised how helpless she felt inside her body. She wanted to help her husband better understand the household chores that needed doing. Mr Casutt was also touched. Now, he could empathize with her: how deprived of dignity his wife must feel! The illness degraded her—and he, too, had contributed to her plight. Reconciliation happened and their reunion lasted several weeks.

76 *The five-phase reconciliation process*

Four months later, Mrs Casutt grew desperate again. Her (progressive) illness had surfaced the same conflicts (crisis). Talking soothed her and she could cry (experience of hope). A week later she was readmitted, and events now overtook one another. One afternoon, she felt spiritually nurtured during music-assisted relaxation. In the evening, her doctor came round and observed that she had fallen into another crisis. And yet, once more, spending time with me gave her courage. She expressed "a longing for peace, which arose exactly at that moment, near death" (experience of hope). It lasted. The next day, she also told the nurses about her hope for peace. Their esteem did her good. She was able to cry. The next day, she felt reconciled with her husband, as several nurses observed, and yet no one quite knew why. Mrs Casutt only uttered the words "Yes—finding meaning— peace." The point of dying drew closer and closer …

The next day, Mrs Casutt had regained some strength: she decided to also tackle the conflict with her mother. It wasn't right, after all, that her mother had no idea that her daughter would soon die. Once more, Mrs Casutt's decision took effect: it made her cheerful. I arranged the visit—and her mother arrived an hour later. Before we entered the room, I told Mrs Casutt's mother and sister out in the hall about the illness and that death was imminent. I offered no time for protest. Time was too precious. Now was a chance for reunion. Mother and sister nodded and entered the room with me. Mrs Casutt's husband was also present. I stood between Mrs Casutt and her mother. The dying woman felt protected by my presence and her husband's. Encounter took place. I instructed Mrs Casutt's mother several times how to touch her daughter and how not. She shouldn't draw too close, even if her daughter was dying. Every time her mother or sister touched her, I protected the patient. Mrs Casutt said "Thank you" or "Ahhh." Her mother heard these words and cried. Her sister intuitively did things right. Then, we stood in a circle and held hands. Would Mrs Casutt accept a blessing ritual? I asked this question deliberately amid the strained family atmosphere, looking for a spiritual solution to the spiritual problem. "Yes." Mother and daughter were both crying. I prayed: "God, Mrs Casutt loved you so much. Please be with her now, protect and warm her during her final transition. Please be with all of us in that place where we will miss Beatrice (Casutt) so much." Mother and sister left again, deeply moved.

Two nights later, Mrs. Casutt had another crisis. Why did she have to see her mother and sister again? (They had said they would return later that day.) I replied that I could understand her. But her mother and

The five-phase reconciliation process 77

sister needed some support after the shock of hearing that she would soon be dying. I assured Mrs Casutt that I would only allow a short visit, five minutes each. Did she agree? She nodded and felt hopeful. Two hours later, I was present when her mother visited, then her sister. Everything went well. Mother and daughter shook hands without saying a word—for a full five minutes, wholeheartedly. Farewell. Tears.

The next day, another, albeit different kind of crisis occurred. Why couldn't she die? Mrs Casutt was angry at God and herself. Continuing to live in this situation made no sense! I confronted her: death did not happen at will, nor would that be in her best interest. But she could contribute much to her well-being by saying "yes." How should she do that, she asked. I showed her a breathing exercise. During the ensuing music-assisted relaxation, she found hope. She felt "devotion" and found her own way of saying "yes." Half an hour later, she had decided: she wanted to practise saying "yes" and to enter into dialogue with God. Once more, her decision made her happy. Another half an hour later, she felt deeply at peace with herself. She stammered the words "finding meaning" and had fewer symptoms. The nurses observed that Mrs Casutt practised saying "yes" all night, whenever she awoke briefly. The next day, surprisingly quickly, she became somnolent. Only hours later, she died—gasping for breath and helped by appropriate medication—yet very peacefully. I entered her room: she was departing and said "gooood."

So much for the impact of the decision. Under which aspects do decisions occur? Our questionnaire listed the following subcategories (Table 3.4).

Table 3.4 Decision, determination: Patient addresses the issue

Coping	Clarification/resolution now or never, act of volition, willing to engage in a process, accepting therapeutic/spiritual help	☐
Emotional	Empathy, forgiving oneself and others, grieving, saying yes to injury/hurt/the situation	☐
Physical	Going through symptoms, pain, breathing work	☐
Relationships	Discussion with conflicting party *in the presence of* a neutral helper	☐
	Without a helper	☐
	Gesture of reconciliation, making arrangements as a step toward reconciliation	☐
Spiritual	Praying for another person or for one's own openness	☐
	Entering into dialogue with God/fate, bargaining for the sake of a third party	☐

78 *The five-phase reconciliation process*

3.5 Reconciliation and forgiveness

In the face of death, reconciliation and forgiveness are frequent. In our study, 49 out of 50 patients experienced reconciliation at least once, while 45 died in or after the reconciled state. This is almost incredible—and yet not entirely. Closeness to death mobilizes. Closer scrutiny, though, reveals differences that are not merely nuances: reconciliation may be temporary or permanent. It may be an inner process of forgiveness or involve a concrete reunion.

We classified the 12 subcategories in our study into four groups depending on the quality of reconciliation (5d, 5c, 5b, 5a, see Figure 3. Subcategories of Forgiveness/Reconciliation; Phase, Appendix). Let me explain:

Reunion: Twenty-eight patients (of $N = 49$ patients experiencing reconciliation or forgiveness, or both, at least once in the process) also experienced reunion (=subgroup 5d). Encountering the other conflict party under the sign of reconciliation or peace was possible. We observed 69 such instances. What about the others? How else might reconciliation or forgiveness be experienced and observed?

Inner reconciliation and forgiveness: We can achieve reconciliation with someone who refuses contact, not to mention a dead person (e.g., a perpetrator of violence), only within ourselves—by forgiving them. Spiritual reconciliation manifests in many ways, both emotionally and spiritually. It occurs—often simultaneously—with another person, with oneself, and with God. In our study, we needed several subcategories to capture such spiritual reconciliation even approximately. We observed this in 46 patients, in whom the most frequent subcategory was "reconciled, trusting, free, capable of love, flowing" (73 times in 31 patients). Yet neither were patients rare who made peace with God and destiny in a new way, who expressed meaning, or who called themselves "newly religious" (55 times in 24 patients). Even symptom alleviation could be clearly related to a reconciliation event (56 times in 30 patients). Apart from the 28 patients with whom reunion occurred besides inner reconciliation, another 13 patients experienced such inner reconciliation and forgiveness at least once (=subgroup 5c; $N = 49$).

Live and let live: Two people whose chemistry is not really favorable, yet who are both willing to reconcile, may decide to "live and let live," that is, to achieve a truce of sorts. In our study, this happened with another 4 patients, who could neither meet the other person again nor achieve inner reconciliation or forgiveness (=subgroup 5b; $N = 49$).

Release and scapegoating: One particular phenomenon—venting one's anger and unburdening oneself at the expense of a scapegoat—needs

The five-phase reconciliation process   79

closer examination. Is this reconciliation? In the hospital setting, family dynamics may relax at the expense of the attending physician. For instance, all of sudden, everyone agrees that *he* or *she* has not administered cancer treatment at the right time and has sown discord in the family by diagnosing a loved one as incurable. Therapists and nursing staff are also scapegoated, though less frequently. Venting brings relief. We therefore included this phenomenon in our reconciliation categories. In our study, 16 patients experienced release or relief by scapegoating someone else, for instance, a professional at least once, 3 patients even twice. In 4 patients, nothing else (e.g., reunion, inner reconciliation, live and let live) occurred or was observed (=subgroup 5a; $N = 49$). However, relief at the expense of a scapegoat was mostly only temporary, or what Roman Siebenrock, our theological expert, called "pseudo-reconciliation."[7]

Which or "how much" reconciliation or forgiveness, or both, may we hope for in dying? I have often been asked this question, or rather its opposite: is there no partial reconciliation and forgiveness? Reconciliation and forgiveness can only take place within us if fully realized. They are never partial. They may be momentary but are not for the half-hearted. Every reconciled moment contains full reconciliation. In particular the quality of forgiveness—a well-rounded state in which things begin to flow again—helps us understand this. Forgiveness takes place or it does not. It is precisely in dying that we may hope for a wholehearted "yes," which we are given both from within and from without. Never so much as in dying do we experience a category change. Our forgiveness (and whenever possible our reconciliation and reunion) enable us to embrace the challenge of categorical change and vice versa: they are also the gift that arises from change.

Sister Miriam was living in a monastic community. She had metastatic colorectal cancer. Usually, her prayers, spirituality, and recalling a near-death experience, wherein she saw a light after an accident, helped her. Sometimes, however, nothing helped. We met while she was going through a crisis. Her pain and symptoms escalated. She had come to see me as an outpatient, but now had to be admitted as an inpatient. She said: "I'm guilty." I didn't believe her and instead observed a strong self-hatred. Her arm was bandaged to protect her festering, self-inflicted bite wounds. What was troubling Sister Miriam? Our body perception exercises were a gentle attempt to experience a different approach to herself: she could feel her bowels, which wouldn't empty. Here sat her fear, she said. Feeling this, and finding words, did her good (experience of

80 *The five-phase reconciliation process*

hope). She wanted to increase her body awareness in the future. Had she ignored her needs up until now? Sister Miriam returned home.

Two days later, she was hospitalized. The nurses said that she refused everything, wished to rest, was cynical and offended, and said that everything was pointless. One nurse noted (on the observation chart) that unreconciledness was indirectly an issue in Sister Miriam's case. She recorded semi-conscious denial. Noon the following day: crisis. She would love to bite her arm, but it was protected with bandages. A little later, she felt forlorn, indicating that she had probably drawn closer to herself. She had been lonely already as a child. Her father, who was suffering from dementia, had worn exhibitionist underwear when she was a toddler. She screamed, fell silent, and wept. I looked at her concerned: What was her body silently carrying around? She didn't know, and yet she did: after she was born, her father developed strange sexual behaviour ... She grew dizzy. Everything was black, leaving her unable to cope with herself. "Not even God helps! She went back to bed exhausted. I visited her again in the evening. Music-assisted relaxation gave her hope. She cried. Again I looked at her concerned. She felt appreciated and tired. She slept long and deeply.

The next day, Sister Miriam took a first decision: she wanted to forgive and said quietly that she also wished to pray for her father. During music-assisted relaxation accompanied by a monochord, I sang the song of Brother Klaus for her. She heard it and quietly hummed the tune. Her decision almost made her cheerful. Her fatigue persisted. Sister Miriam quickly began approaching death. She grew increasingly bleary. Would this help her?

The next day I played the monochord again. Her experience grew intense: "... there is light, like back then ... like Moses and the burning bush. God is there, but I can't see him." She dozed off and, whispering, continued her thought: "I can only feel him (God) with my back. How strange." She couldn't recall the passage in which Moses only experienced God from behind, yet was touched when I read it to her: "The Lord continued: 'See, there is a place by me where you shall stand on the rock; and while my glory passes by I will put you in a cleft of the rock, and I will cover you with my hand until I have passed by; then I will take away my hand, and you shall see my back; but my face shall not be seen'" (Ex 33:21–23). The image gave Sister Miriam hope, also considering her father's story, she said, and dozed off again.

The five-phase reconciliation process 81

The next day, her sense of crisis recurred. It was all her fault anyway. She was to blame for the incest … . But she lacked the strength to bite and scream. I didn't reach her inwardly until the following day. I touched her hand: "Sister Miriam, can you hear me? It's important." She nodded. She allowed me to broach her self-disparagement. Did her self-hatred have a particular place in her body? She pointed to her arm and, despite her fatigue, tossed her head with amazing strength. Was there another place where she felt loved? She cried and fell silent. I waited and repeated my question: there was no such place, she replied. Did God have a place inside her? She thought for a while and pointed to her chest. I invited her to breathe and to feel her arm and chest … and her intestine. This visibly did her good. She grew calmer and, surprisingly, more awake. She said she longed for peace and reconciliation now that she was so close to death. But also for hope (experience of hope).

Several days later, she decided a second time to tackle the subject. She wanted to resolve matters. She did the same breathing exercise, now more alertly, more consciously, and with the invitation to say "yes" when she exhaled. As if she were showing herself to God in prayer. "Yes—God—Yes—Miriam—Yes." The exercise obviously challenged her deep down: she was sleepy for the rest of the day. Next day at 10 o'clock, she was again caught up in her hurt and symptoms. She wept. I was sent for. I entered her room and played the monochord, whose sound reached her: already after twenty minutes, she said calmly, "it's going to be alright" (experience of hope), and nodded off again.

Two days later, she was more awake and re-experienced hope: time and again, she said, almost tenderly, to the sounds of the monochord: "Miriam, Mi-ri-am." I was impressed. What made this impulse possible? When she said goodbye, she expressed her "hope for reconciliation." I praised her experience and said that self-reconciliation was probably most important (!) in her case, and the gateway to everything else. Merely thirty minutes later, she decided to repeat the breathing exercise, in order to forgive herself and her parents. "Even mother … ." Then: "Can I do that?" Pause. "Can't I do it?" Pause. Sister Miriam struggled. Decision is struggle. I was simply there, holding her until she managed to utter "yesssss" into emptiness. Music kept helping her and, for twenty minutes, she repeated saying "yes." Her closeness to death probably helped her. She grew peaceful (reconciliation) and tired. Two days later, she repeated saying "yes": once more, she decided to forgive;

82 *The five-phase reconciliation process*

saying "yes" to another breathing exercise. This time, however, her intestine and arm hurt—as if she also had to go through her symptoms. Her arm grew hot and then cooler again. Her intestine made noises and relaxed again. "Yes … ." Again, she found inner peace, this time combined with pain relief. "… oh, good" (reconciliation). Fatigue.

To our surprise, the feeling of reconciliation persisted. She also had fewer symptoms and needed less medication. I could only attribute this to her closeness to death, and probably to (an invisible) grace. Sister Miriam said quietly, "even doggedness is allowed." Did she mean her biting, her self-destructiveness? She didn't answer, which was probably unnecessary for her process. Now that her symptoms were stable at a low level, she was transferred to a hospice, where she stayed—seemingly satisfied—for three weeks. I visited her. She was happy, but spoke little. "Good." Her arm was no longer an issue. She sometimes saw her fellow sisters. Her mother visited once (even that was possible) and so did her dementia-stricken father. On both occasions, she said: it was fine, no longer important. She died peacefully in the presence of her mother. —A few weeks later, her father, who had been suffering from dementia for years, also died: unexpectedly and quietly. Had any of his daughter's reconciliation reached him?

Notes

1 For other models, see Sections 1.6, 2.6, 2.11, and 2.12.

2 Awareness of nearing death was a criterion for inclusion in our study. These patients no longer thought they would live for several years, but merely for "a few months, weeks, or days." Even in cases where data were collected for almost two years, patients had first discussed their short life expectancy with the treating physician. It is impossible to exactly predict the course of a disease (possibility of complications; responding better or worse to drug therapy, etc.).

3 Numbering (1–100) was deliberately random, i.e., higher numbering occurred in 50 patients.

4 Interestingly, Mr. Ladner used the word "Habakuk," which in Swiss dialect means nonsense or gibberish. He did not know that Habakkuk is one of the prophetic books in the Bible.

5 The results of this study were first published in Renz et al. (2020), Forgiveness and reconciliation processes in dying patients with cancer https://doi.org/10.1177/1049909119867675

6 The essence of freedom is not the freedom of choice, but taking final responsibility and decision: "… to understand that the freedom of self-disposal, of personal autonomy, is a freedom in relation to the subject as a

The five-phase reconciliation process   83

whole, an ultimate freedom, and a freedom that is exercised in a free and absolute yes or no towards that whereupon and wherefrom of transcendence that we call 'God'" (Rahner, 1976/2005, p. 97).

7 Only 3 of the 16 patients who vented at least once at the expense of a scapegoat died hours or days later. Another 3 patients were among those who achieved reconciliation once (i.e., pseudo-reconciliation), but then returned to denial and died unreconciled. After venting and scapegoating, two patients were classed in the category of "live and let live." The remaining 8 patients continued as follows: 1 with denial; 5 with a crisis followed by an experience of hope; and 2 proceeded directly to an experience of hope. All these 8 patients eventually found their way into profound reconciliation and reunion (see Mr. Ladner, Section 3.2, Figure 1, Appendix).

4 It happens where regret and grace meet

Let me conclude with a twofold plea: for regret and for the awareness that, as human beings, we need grace.

In our study, which factors most enabled genuine reconciliation and forgiveness? As observed, these were experiences of hope (see Section 3.3)—but sometimes also deep spiritual experiences and in particular near-death experiences. Spirituality and religiosity, insofar as they appeared neither dogmatic nor self-righteous, seemed to slightly facilitate reconciliation and forgiveness processes.[1] We can and ought to understand this as "experience-based spirituality or religiosity." When physicians ask me what helps people to die well, I usually think of deep spiritual experiences. While we are neither able to optimize nor make dying happen at will, deep spiritual experiences help us from within. This is also true for reconciliation and forgiveness processes that we undergo on our path toward dying.

And yet, other factors also played a role in our study. Among those patients who described themselves as neither religious nor spiritual, many had sought genuine reconciliation and were able to experience reunion. What was their secret? Six of these 10 non-religious patients experienced a high quality of reconciliation and explicitly mentioned that deep relationships helped them.

Where do spiritual experiences, on the one hand, and deep relationships, on the other, meet? What do these two factors have in common? It is the ability, or the experience, to engage with, to let oneself be touched by, to open ourselves up to a real or transcendent Thou, yet also to our deepest self. It makes sense that such engagement is conducive to reconciliation and forgiveness: these are relational processes and concern all dimensions of connectedness.

The ability to engage with deep relationships and let oneself be touched by another person or by God also entails regret and sometimes even remorse. In our study, no factor favored reconciliation and

DOI: 10.4324/9781003310907-5

It happens where regret and grace meet 85

forgiveness processes quite as much as when patients regretted their guilt or repented. But why?—If I regret, I draw closer to my victim's suffering, perhaps even closer than to my own. In any case, regret is what *we* or one side can bring to the process. It is also what a deep relationship, hope, or spiritual experience can get us to do:

> *One woman described her near-death experience with a single word: remorse. It summed up all that mattered. She said: "I'd like to love those I know and those that I don't know more than I have. I'd like to approach others, things, and myself more consciously even when I'm troubled." Remorse also included her gratitude: she was grateful that she had been given the chance for a new beginning. Having regretted and repented, she was able to create her life anew, including more self-discipline and more self-reconciliation. She experienced remorse as "honest." She was also impressed that people had since looked her straight in the eye more than before. She felt looked at and loved.*

> *A year later, I met this woman again. She was well. Her remorse was followed by "process work": spiritual work, peace processes. She did not explicitly mention "reconciliation" and "forgiveness," even if they were in the air.*

> *Our conversation also affected me: my understanding of near-death experiences in general, as well as of my own formative spiritual experiences, had shifted: since then every account or description implicitly contains the word regret. My thinking now adds that word to every account.*

Regret, awareness of guilt, and sometimes remorse stand on the one side, that of the remorseful and guilty person. Which words correspond to them? Which reply might redeem the regretting person? We may it call grace, gift, love, clemency, compassion, or mercy. They all are gifts of deep relationships or of life itself. They come from outside or from deep inside. Our awareness of guilt, our regret, and our hope for redemption lie on the one side and mercifulness on the other. In between occur reconciliation and forgiveness. They are a matter of atmosphere and happen between "time and timelessness," "place and placelessness." This explains why we can learn these processes from the dying. Reconciliation and forgiveness become possible in terms of death or ultimacy. This is the vantage point from which they need to be considered.

86 *It happens where regret and grace meet*

No matter who or what stands on the other side of the regretting person—another person, death, life, and God Himself: forgiveness, reconciliation, and peace are gifts.

Forgiveness[2]

I know not what it was
Someone or *something*,
that destroyed me,
at the time, and time and again.
I know not what it is
Someone or *something*,
that asks me,
for love, gentleness, and forgiveness
I know not what it is,
Someone or *something*,
it says—, I say: Yes,
and strangely: yes is my freedom and source.
Monika Renz, September 2015

Notes

1 Again, see Renz et al. (2020), Forgiveness and reconciliation processes in dying patients with cancer: https://doi.org/10.1177/1049909119867675
2 I wrote this poem after suffering two accidents. It was initially titled "Prägung" "Imprinting" (Renz, 2017). Now, I might as well call it "forgiveness."

References

Ali, A. Y. (1967). *The Holy Qur'an: English Translation, Commentary, and Notes with full Arabic Text (English and Arabic Edition)*. New Delhi: Kitab Bhavan.

Arendt, H. (1958). *The Human Condition.* Chicago: University of Chicago Press.

Ausländer, R. (1986). *Wieder ein Tag aus Glut und Wind: Gedichte 1980–1982.* Frankfurt a.M.: S. Fischer.

Bauer, J. (2010). Vorwort. In K. Stauss (ed.), *Die heilende Kraft der Vergebung: die sieben Phasen spirituell-therapeutischer Vergebungs- und Versöhnungsarbeit* (4th ed., pp. 11–15). München: Kösel.

Cancik, H., Gladigow, B., & Laubscher, M. S. (1988). *Handbuch religionswissenschaftlicher Grundbegriffe*. Stuttgart: W. Kohlhammer.

De Waal, F. (2000). The First Kiss: Foundations of Conflict Resolution Research in Animals. In F. Aureli & F. de Waal (eds.), *Natural conflict resolution* (pp. 15–33). Berkeley: University of California Press.

Derrida, J. (2001). *On Cosmopolitanism and Forgiveness*. London: Routledge.

Drewermann, E. (1991). Vergeben, weil mir vergeben worden ist. In A. Heller (ed.). *Was uns Zukunft gibt vom Reichtum des Lebens* Olten: Walter.

Eliade, M. (1993). *The Encyclopedia of Religion*. London: Macmillan.

Enright, R. D. (2001). *Forgiveness is a Choice*. Washington, D.C.: APA Books.

Enright, R. D., & Fitzgibbons, R. P. (2015). *Forgiveness Therapy: An Empirical Guide for Resolving Anger and Restoring Hope*. Washington, D.C.: American Psychological Association.

Galtung, J. (1998). Re: After violence: 3R, Reconstruction, Reconciliation, Resolution. Coping with Visible and Invisible Effects of War and Violence. Retrieved from https://numerons.files.wordpress.com/2012/04/2coping-with-visible-and-invisible-effects-of-war-and-violence.pdf

Gerl-Falkovitz, H.-B. (2008). *Verzeihung des Unverzeihlichen? Ausflüge in Landschaften der Schuld und der Vergebung*. Vienna: Styria.

Grün, A., & Karimi, M. (2019). Wie zu leben wäre: Spirituelle Lebenskunst. In R. Walter (ed.). *Im Herzen der Spiritualität*. Freiburg i.Br.: Herder.

Hell, D. (2018). *Lob der Scham: nur wer sich achtet, kann sich schämen*. Giessen: Psychosozial Verlag.

88 References

Herman, J. (2015). *Trauma and Recovery: The Aftermath of Violence—from Domestic Abuse to Political Terror*. New York, NY: Basic Books.

Herzog, A. (2017). Was ist Versöhnung, was nicht? Ein Überblick. In F. v. Tiedemann (ed.), *Versöhnungsprozesse in der Paartherapie: ein Handbuch für die paartherapeutische Praxis* (pp. 17–40). Paderborn: Junfermann.

Huber, M. (2003). *Trauma und die Folgen*. Paderborn: Junfermann.

Jampolsky, G. (1999). *Forgiveness: The Greatest Healer of All*. Hillsboro, OR: Beyond Words Publisher.

Jung, C. G. (1957–1992). Psychology and religion, West and East. In M. Fordham, G. Adler, & H. Read (eds.). *Collected Works* (Vol. 1–20). London: Routledge.

Kübler-Ross, E. (1969). *On Death and Dying*. New York, NY: Macmillan.

Lederach, J. P. (1997). *Building Peace: Sustainable Reconciliation in Divided Societies*. Washington, D.C.: United States Institute of Peace.

Lehnen, H., Maiwald, R., Gembruch, U., & Zechner, U. (2010). Epigenetische Aspekte der fetalen und perinatalen Programmierung. *Frauenarzt, 51*, 542–547. Retrieved from http://www.med.uni-magdeburg.de/unimagdeburg_mm/Downloads/Kliniken/KGYN/Fortbildungen/21_10_2010-p-9883.pdf

Lommel, P. van. (2010). *Consciousness Beyond Life: The Science of the Neardeath Experience*. New York, NY: HarperOne.

McCullough, M. E. (2008). *Beyond Revenge: The Evolution of the Forgiveness Instinct*. San Francisco, CA: Jossey-Bass.

Mieth, D., & Mieth, I. (2019). *Sterben und Lieben: Selbstbestimmung bis zuletzt*. Freiburg i.Br.: Herder.

Müller-Fahrenholz, G. (1996). *Vergebung macht frei: Vorschläge für eine Theologie der Versöhnung*. Frankfurt a.M.: Lembeck.

Nietzsche, F. (2003). *Thus Spoke Zarathustra: a Book for All and None* (T. Wayne, transl.). New York, NY: Algora (Originally published in 1883).

Nowak, M. A. (2006). *Evolutionary Dynamics: Exploring the Equations of Life*. Cambridge, MA: Belknap Press.

Rahner, K. (2005). *Foundations of Christian Faith: An Introduction to the Idea of Christianity* (W. V. Dych, transl.). New York, NY: Seabury Press. (Originally published in 1976).

Renz, M. (2015). *Dying: A Transition* (M. Kyburz, with J. Peck, transl.). In K. Anderson (ed.) *End-of-Life Care: A Series*. New York: Columbia University Press.

Renz, M. (2016). *Hope and Grace: Spiritual Experiences in Severe Distress, Illness and Dying* (M. Kyburz, transl.). London: Jessica Kingsley Publishes.

Renz, M. (2017). *Erlösung aus Prägung: ein neues Verständnis von Heilung. Theologie und Psychologie im Gespräch* (2nd revised ed.). Paderborn: Junfermann.

Renz, M. (2020). *Jesus the Mystic: Pathways to Spiritual Care* (M. Kyburz, transl.). Chestnut Ridge, NY: Crossroad Publishing Company.

References 89

Renz, M. (2022). *Fear and Primordial Trust: From Becoming an Ego to Becoming Whole* (M. Kyburz, transl.). London: Routledge.

Renz, M., Bueche, D., Reichmuth, O., Schuett Mao, M., Renz, U., Siebenrock, R., & Strasser, F. (2020). Forgiveness and reconciliation processes in dying patients with cancer. *American Journal of Hospice & Palliative Care, 37*(3), 222–234. https://doi.org/10.1177/1049909119867675

Renz, M., Reichmuth, O., Bueche, D., Traichel, B., Schuett Mao, M., Cerny, T., & Strasser, F. (2018). Fear, Pain, Denial, and Spiritual Experiences in Dying Processes. *American Journal of Hospice and Palliative Care, 35*(3), 478–491. Retrieved from https://www.ncbi.nlm.nih.gov/pmc/articles/PMC5794111/

Renz, M., Schuett Mao, M., Bueche, D., Cerny, T., & Strasser, F. (2013). Dying is a transition. *American Journal of Hospice and Palliative Care, 30*(3), 283–290. https://doi.org/10.1177/1049909112451868

Rohr, R. (2012). *Falling Upward: Spirituality for the Two Halves of Life*. San Francisco, CA: Jossey-Bass.

Schenker, A. (2001). *Knecht und Lamm Gottes: (Jesaja 53). Übernahme von Schuld im Horizont der Gottesknechtlieder*. Stuttgart: Katholisches Bibelwerk.

Stauss, K. (2010). *Die heilende Kraft der Vergebung: die sieben Phasen spirituell-therapeutischer Vergebungs- und Versöhnungsarbeit* (4th ed.). München: Kösel.

Steenwyk van, G., Roszkowski, M., Manuella, F., Franklin, T. B., & Mansuy, I. M. (2018). Transgenerational inheritance of behavioral and metabolic effects of paternal exposure to traumatic stress in early postnatal life: evidence in the 4th generation. *Environmental Epigenetics, 4*(2), dvy023. Retrieved from https://www.ncbi.nlm.nih.gov/pubmed/30349741. doi:10.1093/eep/dvy023

The Bible: New Revised Standard Version. (1995). New York, NY: National Council of the Churches of Christ in the United States of America.

Thomas, C. A. (2004). *At Hell's Gate: A Soldier's Journey from War to Peace*. Boston: Shambhala Publications.

Tiedemann, F. von (2017). Wenn die Seele ruhig wird: ein strukturiertes Vorgehen zur Anleitung von Versöhnungsprozessen in der Paartherapie. In F. von Tiedemann (ed.), *Versöhnungsprozesse in der Paartherapie: ein Handbuch für die Praxis* (pp. 65–203). Paderborn: Junfermann.

Tietz, C. (2005). *Freiheit zu sich selbst: Entfaltung eines christlichen Begriffs von Selbstannahme* (Zugl. Tübingen, Univ, Habil -Schr, 2004). Göttingen: Vandenhoeck & Ruprecht.

Tutu, D., & Tutu, M. (2014). *The Book of Forgiving: The Fourfold Path for Healing Ourselves and Our World*. New York, NY: HarperOne.

Unger, A. (2019). *Vergebung: eine Spurensuche*. Freiburg i.Br.: Herder.

Wilbertz, N. (2017). Wenn der Versöhnungsprozess stagniert: zum Umgang mit blockierenden, aus der Kindheit stammenden Verhaltensmustern. In F. von Tiedemann (ed.), *Versöhnungsprozesse in der Paartherapie: ein Handbuch für die Praxis* (pp. 205–240). Paderborn: Junfermann.

Wirtz, U. (2014). *Trauma and Beyond: The Mystery of Transformation*. New Orleans, LA: Spring Journal Books.

90   References

Wolfers, M. (2013). *Die Kraft des Vergebens: wie wir Kränkungen überwinden und neu lebendig werden* (2nd ed.). Freiburg: Herder.

Worthington, E. L. (2006). *Forgiveness and Reconciliation: Theory and Application.* London: Routledge.

Worthington, E. L., & Sandage, S. J. (2016). *Forgiveness and Spirituality in Psychotherapy: a Relational Approach.* Washington: American Psychological Association.

Appendix

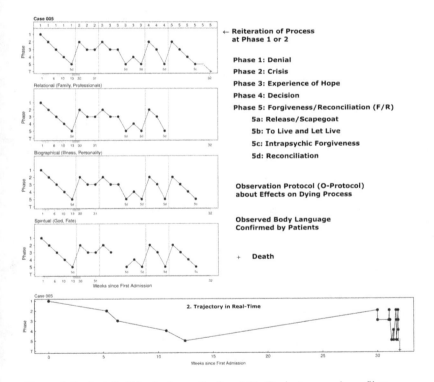

Figure 1 Patient 5: (Mr. Ladner, Section 3.2): Trajectory and conflicts.

92 Appendix

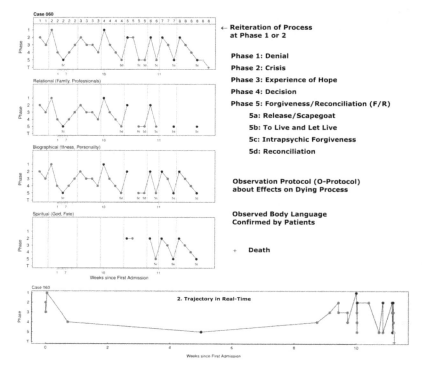

Figure 2 Patient 60: (Mrs Casutt, Section 3.4): Trajectory and conflicts.

Appendix 93

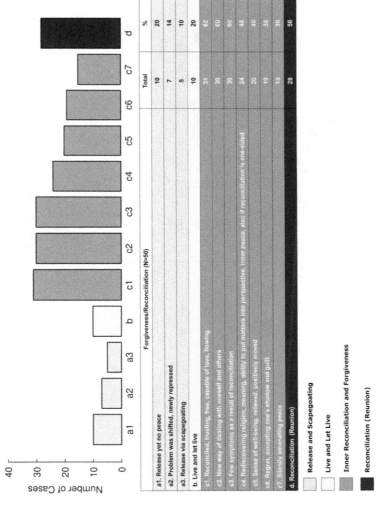

Figure 3 Subcategories of forgiveness/reconciliation (Phase 5).

94 *Appendix*

Table 1 Characteristics of sample

	Deceased Patients (N = 50)	
Male	31	62%
Female	19	38%
Age		
38–50	5	10%
51–70	30	60%
71–87	15	30%
Religious affiliation		
Protestant	18	36%
Catholics	21	42%
Free protestant churches	2	4%
Other Christian denominations	1	2%
No religious tradition	8	16%
Religious/spiritual attitude		
I am religious/I like to pray	7	14%
I am spiritual/I like to meditate	3	6%
I am religious and spiritual	9	18%
I am only generally interested in R/S	15	30%
I am neither religious nor spiritual	16	32%
Experiences and coping strategies		
I had a near-death/deep spiritual experience	7	14%
Repression helps me	27	54%
Deep relationships help me	28	56%

Index

Page numbers followed by f indicate figure and by t indicate table

Acceptance, victims and 49
Alcoholics Anonymous (AA), Twelve
    Step Program of 58–59
Anger 40, 49, 57
Anselm of Canterbury's Theory of
    Satisfaction 59
Arendt, Hannah 30
as-Sadat, Anwar 1
Augustinus, Aurelius 2
Avoidance; *see* Denial

Bauer, Joachim 7
Buber, Martin 26
Buddhism, compassion and 6

Christianity; *see also* Eternal Thou;
    Guilt
    forgiveness in 6, 52
    hope 72
    repentance 54
Christian terms, forgiveness and
    reconciliation in 2
Conflict, as relationship problem
    25–29
Conscious avoidance 66
Conscious realization
    forgiveness, reconciliation and
      32–35
    development of human
      consciousness 27–28

Coping
    with life, victims and experiences
      of 50
    reconciliation manifestation by
      66t, 71, 73t, 77t
Crisis (phase) 2
    denial or avoidance *vs.* 69
    reconciliation manifestation by
      67–71, 71t, 73t, 77t

Death
    forgiveness, reconciliation and
      1–2, 18–22, 69, 79
    repentance and 54–55
Decision
    forgiveness as 55–58
    reconciliation and (phase 5)
      74–77, 77t
Denial or avoidance (phase 1)
    crisis *vs.* 69
    reconciliation and 64–67, 66t
de Waal, Frans 7
Drewermann, Eugen 23
Dying patients with cancer, study of;
    see also Patient 5; Patient 60
    characteristics of sample 13,
      72, 94t
    forgiveness and reconciliation
      processes in 8–11
    forgiveness/reconciliation,

96 *Index*

subcategories of
(phase 5) 93f
Dying processes, shadow integration
of 51

Emotional, reconciliation manifestation
by 66t, 71t, 73t, 77t
Empathy
new, forgiveness, reconciliation
and 35–39
with partner 56
End-of-life carers, examples of 19–22
Endure, victims and help to 49
Enright, Robert D. 57
Enright four phases for
forgiveness 57
Eternal Thou, relationship with
26–29, 33–34;
see also Christianity
Exhaustion-induced forgiveness 18

Fear 40
Five-phase model of forgiveness/
reconciliation 9
Forgiveness; *see also* Dying patients
with cancer; Reconciliation
after category change 30–32
in Christian terms 2
conscious realization, post-
maturation, truth finding
and 32–35
death and 69
as decision 55–58
as expression of strength 23–24
forgiveness/reconciliation (phase
5), subcategories of 93f
freedom and 14–16
generosity to forgive, victims and
49–50
guilt and 25–26; *see also* (Guilt)
historical and religio-historical
backgrounds of 5–8
meaning of 3–4
mindset, change in 30–32, 52, 78
motivation and 17–18
new empathy and 35–39

overcoming hard times 39–40
possibility of 32
reconciliation *vs.* 2, 3–4
study in dying patients with cancer
8–11; *see also* (Dying patients)
third parties and 42–45
*Forgiveness: The Greatest Healer
of All* (Jampolsky) 17
Freedom and peace, victims and path
to 52
Futility 25

Gandhi, Mahatma 23
Gayle, Aba 52
Generosity to forgive, victims and
49–50
Gerl-Falkovitz, Hanna-Barbara 28–29
Gift and given, forgiveness and 3
Guilt 38, 58–62
Gurkasch, Dieter 53

Happiness, victims and experiences
of 52
Hawaiians, reconciliation,
forgiveness and 6
Help to endure, victims and 49
Herzog, Andrea 23
Historiography, victims and new
51–52
Hope
experiences of forgiveness and
(phase 3) 4, 84
experiences of reconciliation and
(phase 3) 4, 72–74, 73t, 84
Hurt, recalling 56

Individualism; *see* Maturation
Impartial listening 49
Insight, remorse, victims and 52
Islam, forgiveness and 6
I-Thou relationship 26, 29

Jampolsky, Gerald G. 17
*Jesus The Mystic: Pathways to
Spiritual Care*, 2020, 5
Jung, C. G. 5

Index 97

Kor, Eva 52
Kübler-Ross, Elisabeth 65, 66t

Listening, impartial 49
Liturgy of the Eucharist 59–62
Live and let live 78
Lommel, Pim van 7
Luther, Martin 28

Mandela, Nelson 52
Maturation/individualism;
　see conscious realization; Dying
　processes, shadow integration;
　Empathy, new; Overcoming role
　of victim; Shadow work,
　individual victim
McCullough, Michael 6, 7
Mengele, Dr. 52
Mertes, Klaus 49
Mieth, Dietmar 18
Mindset, victims and change in 52
Models, from the perpetrator's
　perspective
　first: Twelve-step Program of
　　Alcoholics Anonymous
　　(AA) 58–59
　second: Liturgy of the Eucharist
　　59–62
Models, of forgiveness as decision
　from the victim's perspective
　55–58
Motivation, forgiveness,
　reconciliation and 17–18

Nietzsche, Friedrich 26

Overcoming role, victims and 50

Patience, victims and 52
Patients, trajectories and case
　vignettes
　Bocca, Mr. 66–67
　Cadisch, Mrs. 19–20
　Camenisch, Mr. 35–37
　Casutt, Mrs. (Patient 60) 74–77
　Halter, Mrs. 42–43
　Hatt, Mrs. 70–71
　Hidegard 15–16

Ladner, Mr. (Patient 5) 68–69
Miriam, Sister 79–92
Moll, Mr. 54
Nauer, Mr. 20–22
Patient 5, trajectory and conflicts
　68, 72, 91f
Patient 60, trajectory and conflicts
　68, 72, 74–75, 92f
Rahel 14–15, 16
Ramadami, Bassam 15–16
Tuner, Mrs. 45–47
Peace and order, reconciliation and
　path to 3
Perpetrators
　need of 52–55
　two models from the perspective
　　of 58–62
　victims and 52
Physical, reconciliation manifestation
　by 66t, 71t, 73t, 77t
Post-maturation, forgiveness,
　reconciliation and 32–35
Privacy and sheltered spaces,
　perpetrators and 55

Rahner, Karl 74
Recognizing suffering, of victims 50
Reconciliation
　after category change 30–32
　in Christian terms 2
　conscious realization, post-
　　maturation, truth finding
　　and 32–35
　death and 69
　as expression of strength 23–24
　five-phase process of 64–82
　forgiveness *vs.* 3–4
　freedom and 14–16
　historical and religio-historical
　　backgrounds of 5–8
　meaning of 1, 3, 4–5
　mindset, change in 30–32, 52, 78
　motivation and 17–18
　as mutual process 40–42
　new empathy and 35–39
　overcoming hard times 39–40
　possibility of 32
　refusal by other side 25

98 *Index*

reunion with the other conflict party 78
study in dying patients with cancer; *see* (Dying patients with cancer)
third parties and 42–45
unilateral 45–48
Relationships
conflict as problem in 25–29
deep 84–85
reconciliation manifestation by 66t, 71t, 73t, 77t
resilience and 42
Release and scapegoating 78–79
Repentance, death and 54–55
Reunion, forgiveness/reconciliation and 78
Rohr, Richard 7

Self-acceptance, victims and 49
Shadow work, individual victim and 51–52
Sheltered spaces, perpetrators and 53
South Africa's Truth Commission 33
Spirituality, reconciliation manifestation by 66t, 71t, 73t, 77t, 84
St. Gallen Cantonal Hospital 4, 8, 10
Strauss, Konrad 25–26, 27, 28, 32
Strength, forgiveness and reconciliation as expression of 23–24

Stress, forgiveness and reduction of 56
Study "Forgiveness and reconciliation processes in dying patients with cancer"; *see* Dying patients with cancer

Third parties, forgiveness, reconciliation and 42–45
Thomas, Claude Anshin 53
Tiedemann, Friederike von 32, 40–42
Trust of others, perpetrators and 55
Truth Commission in South Africa 6
Truth finding, forgiveness, reconciliation and 32–35
Tutu, Desmond 1, 23, 24, 32

Uncovering phase (uncovering anger) 57
Unilateral reconciliation 45–48

Vanier, Jean 49
Versuenen, meaning of 1
Verwicklung (embroilement) 67
Victims, reconciliation and 48–52

Wilbertz, Norbert 41–42
Wilson, William Griffith 58
Wolfers, Melanie 32
Worthington, Everett L. 32, 55
Worthington five phases 56

Printed in the USA
CPSIA information can be obtained
at www.ICGtesting.com
LVHW010932190324
774517LV00003BA/227